100 THINGS THAT PiSS ME OFF

... OR IS IT JUST ME?

ROSS BURNS

ILLUSTRATIONS BY KAZ CLARKE

The illustrations in this book are lovingly dedicated to my father, Maxwell Clarke, who sadly passed away while I was completing them. A lover of funny cartoons, he would have thoroughly enjoyed the humour of this book. I hope I did you proud Dad. – Kaz Clarke

Copyright © 2021 Ross Burns

Illustrations by Karen Clarke: www.planetphoebe.com

ISBN: 978-1-922565-39-6
Published by Vivid Publishing
A division of Fontaine Publishing Group
P.O. Box 948, Fremantle
Western Australia 6959
www.vividpublishing.com.au

 A catalogue record for this book is available from the National Library of Australia

All rights reserved. No part of this publication may be reproduced, stored in a retrieval system or transmitted in any form or by any means, electronic, mechanical, photocopying, recording or otherwise, without the prior written permission of the copyright holder. The information, views, opinions and visuals expressed in this publication are solely those of the author(s) and do not necessarily reflect those of the publisher. The publisher disclaims any liabilities or responsibilities whatsoever for any damages, libel or liabilities arising directly or indirectly from the contents of this publication.

CONTENTS

Welcome to my (grumpy) world ix

1. Trendy bullshit buzzwords 1
2. Fashion and the 'power of clothes' 8
3. Butter gougers 11
4. Fancy can openers: Which way is up? 13
5. The Eleventh Commandment: 'Thou shalt not get the haircut that thou asked and paid for' 16
6. Spray painted toilet bowls 19
7. People who don't walk on the left-hand side of the footpath 21
8. What the hell is a 'life coach'? 24
9. Crowds: Two people, including me 27
10. Snakes 30
11. Radio shock jocks: A waste of valuable oxygen 33
12. People-spreaders 37
13. The mindless preoccupation with mobile phones ... 41
14. Shit happenings 46
15. Having to bend down and touch my toes 49
16. Hernias and the unwanted duck egg 51
17. Ostentatious weddings: Why do we bother? 54
18. Canberra bashing and what it means for Ulaanbaatar 58

19. Tiptoeing through the tulips: Political correctness gone berserk 61
20. Unsuccessfully eating a pie while driving 66
21. Baby girls' floral headbands: The parental tribute 69
22. Taj Mahal-style McMansions 71
23. Speed bumps and broken teeth 74
24. Small children (and larger ones too) 76
25. Beer that's less than icy cold (and related boutique irritations) 80
26. The relentless quest for instant now-ness 83
27. Mispronounced words 87
28. Having to engage with the community 90
29. What the hell is a 'social commentator'? 93
30. The indiscriminate use of multiple 'woo woos' 96
31. Flies (particularly the blow variety) 99
32. The wearing of baseball caps back-to-front 103
33. Plane travel (and small children on planes) 106
34. Ageism: It's NOT funny 110
35. Clogged straws (paper or plastic – same catastrophic result) 114
36. Politicians 117
37. Slamming doors and shit-for-brains slammers 119
38. Windows rolled down in taxis: The Cat. 5 effect 122
39. Using the present tense to describe past events 125
40. The pogo dance (the up and down jiggy thingy) 127
41. Loud and aggressive people 130
42. Swished hair (left or right – same comical result) 134
43. Stinky perfumes and aftershaves 137

44. The malfunctioning photocopier 139
45. The 'no worries, no dramas, too easy' reassurance ... 143
46. Automatically beginning sentences with 'so' 146
47. The stacks-on-the-mill footy fall down 148
48. Opinions (including/especially mine) 150
49. Power pramming yummy mummies 153
50. The under supply of milk in hotel rooms 157
51. Words like 'gourmet', 'luxury', 'exotic', 'five star', 'paradise' and 'exclusive' 161
52. Having to converse before 11:00 am 164
53. Having to converse at all 167
54. What the hell is a 'relationship coach'? 170
55. Staggeringly thoughtless drivers 174
56. The bullshit job interview question: 'What are your salary expectations?' 178
57. Spasmodic Australian-ness 182
58. 'Unsubscribe' buttons that don't 185
59. Badly behaved shopping trolleys 187
60. Feral kids in shopping trolleys 190
61. People who stand in doorways or two abreast on escalators 192
62. Siri: Why won't she go out with me? 195
63. Bad grammar, misspelling, and email madness 198
64. Flat-packed furniture 201
65. The abuse of social media 204
66. Uncaring lifts 207
67. People who talk to you in uncaring lifts 210
68. Authority – except for the lollypop man 213

69.	Banks	216
70.	Broad beans and related bowel irritants	218
71.	Rubbish advertising: Not happy, Jan!	221
72.	Modern day packaging	224
73.	Over-the-top consumerism	227
74.	The Logies: Who are these people?	230
75.	Grossly disturbing personal habits	233
76.	The 'tall poppy' accusation: Why we get it wrong	237
77.	Comically (un)fascinating fascinators	239
78.	The bowels of Mrs B's handbag	242
79.	Being made to feel like you don't matter	245
80.	Losing an Ashes test cricket series	249
81.	Pusherinners	253
82.	People who involve you in their mobile phone conversation	256
83.	Celebrityism: Who are these people?	259
84.	Tradies who don't front up: 'It was my birthday'	262
85.	People who don't acknowledge your simple act of politeness	264
86.	Knowing bugger all about the new job you just started	267
87.	2.29.42 am and the brain/bladder hostilities	269
88.	Trial by media and the armchair judgment	271
89.	Meetings and the people who attend them	274
90.	The ubiquitous 'coffee traveller'	278
91.	'So, how's your day been so far?'	280
92.	The wanky health and fitness industry	282
93.	Being hopelessly unfit	286

94. People who insist on 'making a statement'	289
95. The unreality of Reality TV	293
96. Foodie wankers: Looking good on TV and being able to boil an egg	296
97. Selfies and grinning gooses	300
98. The grinding humiliation of unemployment	302
99. Catheter tubes and how not to install them	306
100. The performing nose syndrome	309
A final (grumpy) word	312

WELCOME TO MY (GRUMPY) WORLD

It must be galloping old age. Or, I'm just a natural-born grump. Of course, a combination of the two afflictions is guaranteed to unearth a curmudgeon of epic proportions. And, in my case, it most assuredly has.

In my defence, maybe there's a Catch 22 theme I can fall back on here: some men are born grumpy, some men achieve grumpiness and some men have grumpiness thrust upon them. With me, it's surely been the cataclysmic result of all three.

Regardless of the origin, that's me. That's just 'how I roll'. (We'll get to how much buzzwords piss me off in due course.)

Some may call it perverse, but I'm quite content in my grumpiness. Not *happily* grumpy, though. That'd be beyond perverse and, in any case, being a natural-born grump, happiness isn't a concept with which I'm particularly familiar. I simply have a deeply satisfying, almost pride-filled acceptance that I've found my place in the world. My niche. Where I fit in. Where I belong. A space in which I can truly claim to have achieved greatness, if not respectability – but without the effort or gifted-from-birth talent that greatness normally demands.

Yes, I'm a fully paid-up, card-carrying, almost-professional grump. I live in 'Grump House'. In Grump Street. In Grump Town. In Grump World. It's kind of cool and reassuring when you analyse it, rationalise it and break it down into its constituent parts. I'm a tragic 'compartmentaliser' – and occasional bullshit buzzword user.

What you're about to read – and thanks for reading this far by the way: the introduction plus the contents page, a spectacular achievement on your part (not that I really care one way or the other – that's a wonderful, enriching and life-fulfilling side-benefit of being a grump. You don't give a toss what people think of you, or what they think at all. Or, *if* they think at all which, let's face it, many plainly don't). If you read on, good for you. You're a legend. Go you good thing. If you don't, care factor zero. Quite simply, I don't give a flying rat's.

Anyway, if you *do* decide to take the experience to the next level, you won't find any order to the 100 Things That Piss Me Off. The list is just a random collection of, well, a hundred things that piss me off. They're not laid out in any particular priority, or even alphabetically. They've not been collated in a sliding scale of grumpiness. There are no standouts. No mega superstars. No must-haves. They're merely presented in the order in which they popped into my head, reflecting my state of fire-danger grumpiness at the time – very high, severe, extreme or catastrophic.

But you'll notice that each of my grump gripes is rated on a scale of one to one hundred. I thought that would be only fair and reasonable. Perspective in all aspects of life is essential, so I'm constantly reminded. Besides, it saves me having to grumpily write another book: 'Lots of Other Things That I Find Only Marginally, Mildly or Moderately Irritating … Or is it Just *Me*? (Volume One)'.

* * *

Where did this soul-searching 'journey' begin? (Like I mentioned, bullshit buzzwords piss me off in a huge way, as you'll soon discover. I apologise for using one here, but I felt compelled to 'make a statement' about what a deep and contemporary thinker I am.)

It all started just after take-off on a flight from Darwin to Perth in March 2018. Generally speaking, plane travel pisses me off in a major way so I wasn't off to a flying start, but we'll come to that later, too. We'd just been given 'the-Captain-has-turned-off-the-fasten-seat-belt-sign' announcement when Boofhead 1 in the seat in front of me (obviously a serial recliner) propelled his seat backwards to within about five centimetres of my nose. It was a cramped Virgin flight so what would you expect? Of course, I expected nothing. And, typically, was rewarded with even less.

At or about the same time, Boofhead 2 in the seat directly behind me sprang from *his* seat and, to give himself the extra leverage needed to heave his not insubstantial butt into the air, grabbed hold of the top of *my* seat, yanked it backwards, and then, in slingshot fashion, let it go. *Pachoyng*.

The consequence of the contemporaneous co-joining of the actions of couldn't-give-a-stuff Boofheads 1 and 2 was to sandwich me between the two seats, only fractionally avoiding several broken ribs, a punctured lung and other miscellaneous internal injuries.

This escalated my then mildly pissed-off state into wild overdrive, particularly given the now close proximity of the gross and visually disturbing noggin of Boofhead 1, the back of which I was then forced to stare at for the next three and half hours.

The whole sorry event reminded me that many things piss me off, and regularly. I decided to give myself a stern test to while away the boredom which, strangely, I quite enjoy. How many things that piss me off could I list before touching down in Perth? (Sorry, folks, it's just the off-centre way in which my brain operates.)

I managed, comfortably, to make it to 73.

When you 'do the math', that's about one grizzle experience every three minutes. A stupendous accomplishment, I thought, that only a gifted, grumpy few could achieve.

No worries. No dramas. Too easy. (We'll come to *that* little gem later, too.)

I rattled off the other 27, easily cracking the ton, in the course of the trip from Perth to Margaret River*. That's where I live with my partner-in-grumpiness, my long-suffering wife Mrs B. She's nowhere near as inherently grumpy as me, though she works tirelessly to follow my shining example.

For the most part, Mrs B looks on the bright side of life, which is truly amazing given her very dodgy recent medical history. This, in itself, is something that pisses me off to some degree. But, only intermittently, so that irksome idiosyncrasy didn't make it into this anthology. It's barely a blip on the radar in *my* grumpy world.

I look upon Mrs B's general cheeriness as a counter-balance to my very ordinary disposition. A squaring of the ledger you might say. Perspective again. But I do wonder sometimes how we ever got together, let alone how we've have stayed together for well over four decades.

(*By the way, in no way is Margaret River 'Grump Town' as I alluded to earlier. Nothing could be further from the truth. It's a wonderful town full of warm and wonderful people. That was just me being a grizzle-guts, again.)

* * *

As you wander through this book, if you bother to wander at all, you'll notice three blank pages (yeah, ok, you've been short-changed by three per cent – get over it). These aren't accidental omissions, editorial errors or senior moments on my part. The omissions are deliberate. When you come to them, you'll know why. If you can't comprehend my meaning instantly, that'll *really* piss me off. In my view, no commentary is needed on these entries. You can fill in the blanks with your own thoughts if you wish. (A touch of snazzy writer/reader 'interface', so I thought.) I suspect, though, that you'll understand why I've decided not to comment and also choose to leave these three entries untouched. There really isn't anymore that can be said on these three topics that hasn't already been given considerable negative air time, if not flogged completely to death.

Anyway, enjoy.

Or not. I'll only be minimally pissed off if you don't, so my mild level of annoyance isn't likely to make it into Volume Two.

1.
TRENDY BULLSHIT BUZZWORDS

I mentioned earlier that there's no order of priority in my list of 100 Things That Piss Me Off.

Having said that, trendy but meaningless bullshit buzzwords must sit somewhere towards the top. This is a 'biggie' for me and I feel a strong urge to get it off my chest, and quickly.

As periodically fragile human beings, we seem obliged to conjure up all manner of things to provide a measure of reassurance for us in times of uncertainty and unease. When we lose all hope, when life has no meaning, when we simply can't navigate our way out of bed in the morning, we reach for, and then sadly hide behind, buzzword comfort.

For me, though, the experience is pure torture.

When some goose tries to convince me that life – or even making a toasted ham, cheese and tomato sandwich for lunch – is a 'journey', I feel an irresistible urge to wail like a demented banshee.

When I'm beseeched to 'reach out', particularly to those to whom I have less than zero interest in reaching out (which, to be clear, is virtually every other person on the planet), I have an overwhelming self-harm desire to yank my toenails out one by one with a pair of heavy duty pliers.

When some poor, misguided fool begins or ends a sentence with 'going forward' (or, incomprehensibly, manages to do both), I feel as if I've been stabbed in the left eye with a red-hot, super-pointy steel knitting needle.

1. TRENDY BULLSHIT BUZZWORDS

When I'm told to 'make it happen' (usually, and arrogantly, by a bloated corporate-type manager who sees some misplaced significance in the expression and who, invariably, has no clue how to make it happen himself, even if he is a self-proclaimed 'weapon'), I feel like removing *that* person's toenails one by one. With an even less sympathetic pair of pliers.

Explain this to me if you can: why do we appear so obsessed with engaging in a so-called 'national conversation' even with respect to the most minor, marginal or outright irrelevant issue? If we're not having a national conversation about even the most trivial matter (like the state of my dickie lower back), it's obvious we're just not trying hard enough or not taking life as seriously as we should.

Let's be clear. If I 'land' something, it's almost always a fish. When I 'unpack' something, it's almost always a suitcase. If I ever have ducks (though I never will), you can be assured that I'll *never* try to get them in a row. I only ever place words 'on the same page' (even if inappropriately at times – read on). The only form of 'transparency' I'm vaguely interested in is the beer glass variety. The only thing I'm prepared to 'share' on a meaningful basis is my love of grumpiness. The only contributions I'll 'bring to the table' will be pepper and salt and assorted cutlery, and then only grudgingly. Simple principles of ergonomics (and that dickie lower back) prevent me from ever doing any 'heavy lifting'. If I 'smash' something, it'll be an object

I've dropped (I'm crazily clumsy) and will never involve an avocado. I'll only ever 'cut through' a loaf of unsliced bread or a leg of lamb. Being 'empowered' frightens the crap out of me and, in any case, involves way too much effort, as does 'instructional scaffolding' (in effect, so I learnt, teachers helping school children as part of the everyday educational process. But, of course, the buzzword version sounds infinitely more life changing and self-important.)

It's not 'awesome', 'brilliant' or (especially) 'beautiful' when I manage to fill in a simple form correctly (though as we know, many aspiring, but blindingly incompetent politicians can't) or when I recite my full name quickly, or backwards, without too many stuff ups. It's neither 'perfect' nor 'gold' nor 'mint' that I'm capable of placing each of my feet in the correct shoe (we'll get to those unhelpful socks later), and I do not desperately crave 'kudos' for doing so. And, I honestly don't expect anyone to artificially boost my ego by telling me I've 'nailed it' (and high-fiving me) when I remember to brush my teeth before bedtime.

(However, as I get older, I have been known to accidentally 'pop' from time to time but for all the wrong reasons and in all the wrong places with distressingly conspicuous results.)

'Silos' store agricultural products. They have *no* other function. I get absolutely no 'bleisure' from combining business and leisure. (And, FFS, I get bugger all pleasure from 'glamping'.) Whatever 'it' is, I won't 'segue' to it, 'circle back' to it, 'drill down' into it or 'align' myself with it. And, here's some free advice: I'm no one's 'go-to' guy. I wouldn't have a clue how to, who to, when to, what to, why to or where to … go to.

To preserve what small measure of remaining sanity I have, **NEVER** try to 'spit-ball' with me. And, **NEVER** ask me to 'pivot' – I have zero capacity to perform this plainly dreadful task, either physically, figuratively, psychologically, emotionally, socially or any other goddam way. The same applies to the now compulsory 'reset'.

And what, literally, is 'from the get-go' supposed to mean? Does *anyone* know? It makes no grammatical sense whatsoever, even if it has, I understand, some kind of historical or cultural origin. That, of course, doesn't stop us from using it and abusing it from the get-go.

Finally, please don't for one microsecond assume that I have 'passion', even for those things (including buzzwords) that greatly piss me off. It puzzles me why virtually every form of human endeavour these days, from actuarial studies to growing organic mung beans or running a snail farm, must be performed with passion. Isn't it acceptable to just do things with a middling amount of interest? Can't we still feel good about ourselves if we operate fractionally below passion level? I'm making a stand. I refuse to perform *any* activity with passion. Truth be known, I put that theory into practice many years ago.

I'm convinced that those who, sheep-like, use buzzwords (or even common words in a buzzword sense) on a constant, unthinking and indiscriminate basis really have nothing meaningful to say at all, even if they genuinely believe that they're 'shape-shifting' or 'change-making' (or are otherwise 'all over it') when they do so.

In reality, doesn't the use of buzzwords prevent us from saying what we really mean in plain, straightforward and comprehensible English?

My biggest concern with buzzwords, however, apart from the obvious that they're routinely 'invented' by someone who doesn't have the intellect to use perfectly decent and well-chosen words appropriately, is that, sadly, over time, they become part of the lexicon and assume some measure of respectability and legitimacy. (Like, when I've been unconsciously sucked into using them a number of times in this book).

Crap to that.

And a pox on all who use them, trendily.

Phew! That feels so much better! I feel energised. Cleansed. Borderline empowered.

Now for the other ninety-nine. Should be a piece of cake.

SCORE = 96

1. TRENDY BULLSHIT BUZZWORDS

P.S. Of course, I'm very conscious of the fact that 'buzzword' is, itself, a bullshit buzzword. Once again, my apologies. Let me know if there's a non-buzzword alternative.

By the way, 'are you picking up what I'm putting down?'

Yes? 'Look at *you* go!'

2.
FASHION AND THE 'POWER OF CLOTHES'

2. FASHION AND THE 'POWER OF CLOTHES'

Make no mistake. I'm never, thankfully, in imminent danger of making it onto the runway at a Paris fashion show. Maybe Milan or New York in an off year. I know that and everyone who knows me (all three of them) knows that.

Fashion and style trends are matters I've never been remotely interested in and, so I'm told, it shows. T-shirts, jeans, shorts and loose-fitting clothes that are totally unflattering to the human form are still my favoured type of gear. They form a critical part of my own personal, and admittedly very basic, don't-really-care-too-much dress code. My old clothes become my new clothes, and vice versa, on a random rotational (ten to twenty-year life cycle) basis.

It's probably a bloke thing but, when push comes to shove as it often does for me and not too gently, I tend to be dressed by others. I just stand there and cop it, limply and grumpily, and vacate the shop as soon as possible once the ordeal is over and the deal is done – again by others.

Don't hold your breath waiting for me to apologise for not complying with the dress code of the lumber-, metro-, sporno- or uber-sexual. The 'power of clothes' and the closely associated quest to enhance or modify one's personal appearance, quite often bizarrely? Sorry, I just don't get it. Unless someone can convince me otherwise (or Meghan and Kate agree [but certainly not at the same time or in the same room] to wear one of my labels), clothes are placed on this earth to do no more than protect us from the elements and hide our many hideous bits, if I'm any guide.

To put the best possible spin on it, and with all due respect and diplomacy (neither of which I'm known for), I find it curious that many people who go out of their way to enhance their appearance quite often unintentionally achieve the complete opposite.

To me, those who see 'power' in clothes merely render themselves hopelessly, helplessly and haplessly superficial and inadequate. They have my pity, but not my sympathy.

There's more to genuine and valid personal reinvention, or a basic character re-build, than a nifty new pair of designer dacks, ridiculously pointy shoes, spikey-gelled hair, a spiffy shirt that's five sizes too small and a horribly stinky aftershave. Not to mention a brand new, top of the range, replacement partner.

The phrase 'clothes maketh the man' is total rubbish. If it is true, I'm destined for a life on the streets which, if the truth be known, is where I'm heading in any case if I don't change direction, and soon.

SCORE = 94

3.
BUTTER GOUGERS

It's a first-class sign of abysmal laziness.

Or, that you really don't give a stuff for the next person who manages, after way too much unnecessary physical and intellectual effort, to prise the lid off the butter container only to discover the carnage and chaos you've created within.

On any reasonable, semi-civilised standard, butter is, at all stages in its life-span, supposed to resemble the glassy-smooth surface of a tranquil mountain lake, not the pock-marked, bomb-cratered surface of Mars.

I'm exceptionally proud of my Torvill and Dean approach to butter extraction. I calmly glide, gently tease and sensually coax. Surely it's not too difficult to carefully and uniformly encourage the butter out of the container, rather than gouge it out in lumps, clumps and blobs as if you're excavating your way to China.

And, while we're on the subject, if you *must* gouge, at least have the decency to take the leftover toast crumbs, peanut butter, vegemite, strawberry jam, smashed avocado and other miscellaneous and unmentionable grooblies with you as you depart.

If you're a butter gouger, you're not welcome in my house.

If you *have* to be there (and it certainly won't be at *my* invitation), BYO, and take it with you when you leave.

SCORE = 88

4.
FANCY CAN OPENERS: WHICH WAY IS UP?

I can never get the dreadful little fuckers to work. Never.

True confession: I don't even have the faintest idea which way is up or down, as is the case with many other life mysteries, such as how to assemble a standard cardboard packing box. I hand that terrible task on to the nearest modestly intelligent two-year-old. It keeps their dangerous little mitts busy for a few precious minutes, but more on that later.

I *know* it's just me, though.

I don't tinker. I don't potter (though I did take up pottery at one time). I don't mend or repair things. I don't whittle or gadget-fiddle. For good reason, I'd be refused Men's Shed membership. I don't even strum the banjo, play the flute or engage in power yoga in the utility room or, heaven forbid, my 'man cave'. I'm not in the slightest way mechanically minded. I have no concept of how machines work. I can barely distinguish between 'park' and 'reverse' (I mean, *P/R*, what's the difference?) and, to my deep regret and considerable cost, have occasionally mistaken the two – even on a ride-on lawnmower that was positioned at the time in dangerous proximity to a swimming pool.

In short, I'm the sort of person who, for the safety of others and especially small children (not that I care much for *their* welfare), should never be allowed to have a hammer in his hand or be within 100 metres of anything with moving parts. We'll come to lifts and photocopiers later.

No wonder I can't navigate my way around a 'simple' can opener or, needless to say, a new-fangled espresso coffee machine.

By the way, the $1.50 Woolies/Coles/K-Mart/Best & Less can opener varieties don't make my life any easier or more livable. Of course, they're much simpler to operate (even *I* can figure them out after a month or so and a Google search for the most up-to-date instruction manual) but, more often than not, these equally unhelpful objects break in the process because they're made with that very result in mind.

Hence, the cheapness.

SCORE = 90

5.
THE ELEVENTH COMMANDMENT: 'THOU SHALT NOT GET THE HAIRCUT THAT THOU ASKED AND PAID FOR'

5. THE ELEVENTH COMMANDMENT

It's the first tutorial presented at hairdresser training school: 'How to Engage in Tedious, Mind-numbing Conversation with Your Client – as Superficially as Possible (101)'.

As a consequence, our apprentice hairdressers Xander and Marigold (sometimes both together, as individually, they commonly have the attention span of a flea and need to tag-team to get the job done) become easily distracted by their insatiable need for a chat and, invariably, miss the simple and straightforward instructions you gave them just after you declined the usual, insincere, invitation for 'a coffee' or a glass of chilled mineral water.

Listen dudes (let's at least attempt to communicate on their level), *I'll save you the trouble of asking. My day's been crap so far. I'm climbing up the wall from too much caffeine. And no, I can't afford to go away for the weekend. I can barely afford to hang out in my rental hovel. Please cut the chat and just engage in some mild Edward Scissorhands activity and we'll both somehow get through the day.*

To add to the heartache already inflicted, as a bloke, it's only when you arrive home, have a shower and dry and comb your hair that you discover to your horror that, no, our young friends didn't in fact cut your hair the way you clearly directed.

And, in the process, they've left you looking like a nine-year-old neo-Nazi.

And for good measure, you'll be stung with a cost higher than this week's total grocery bill. (In my case, true story.)

SCORE = 88

P.S. The only reason the whole forgettable experience doesn't score higher is that I'm driven back to the time-honoured saying: 'The only difference between a good and a bad haircut is two weeks'.

Shorter or longer, depending on the magnitude of the cock-up.

6.
SPRAY PAINTED TOILET BOWLS

This is one of the grossest personal character flaws known to humankind.

I can, at a pinch (of you know what), forgive the occasional minor stain, discolouration, blemish or inconsequential skid mark. But, when this highly uncouth habit reaches the level of anal graffiti, of major rear-end spray paint proportions, then I must protest in the strongest terms.

Where's your sense of fairness, if not common decency?

Please, have at least some small measure of respect for the next cubicle user or, more importantly, for the poor wretch who has to clean up after you. Been there, done that, and it's not a fun job folks.

The process isn't one of simply flush and go. It only takes a couple of extra seconds to stick around and make a judgment that the bowl hasn't been left resembling the floor of a used cattle pen, and to make one or two minor ceramic adjustments if it has.

Surely it's not too much to leave the bowl in a reasonably sanitary, if not pristine, condition. It's not too big a deal, is it? Not really a show-stopper or game-changer? It involves not much more than interacting with a toilet brush for a few seconds, or pot scourer, depending on the extent of the damage.

C'mon guys. Please, roll up your sleeves a touch and get down and dirty for a few moments. And, remember, the longer you leave it, the harder it gets. Literally.

SCORE = 91

7.
PEOPLE WHO DON'T WALK ON THE LEFT-HAND SIDE OF THE FOOTPATH

I'm unlikely to get much agreement on this one. Certainly, very little empathy. Even less 'traction'. And, bugger all 'engagement'.

Most people, especially those members of the younger generations, simply won't know what I'm talking about.

But I'm old enough to remember (though sometimes not) the time when, as an unspoken and somewhat genteel sign of respect for other pedestrians, people routinely walked on the left-hand side of the footpath. We didn't have to think about it. It was automatic. It was 'as you do'. The magical side effect of this polite acknowledgement was that passers-by rarely bumped into each other.

Now, unfortunately, chaos reigns out there in footpath land and, combined with the mobile phone (surely the work of the Devil) or an out-of-control umbrella or umbrella user, what was once a harmless, very occasionally pleasant, stroll down a pedestrian promenade is now a terrifying ordeal from which you can count yourself extremely fortunate if you escape with merely a black eye and a mouthful of chipped teeth.

And, never lose sight of the additional, unintended consequence that, being confronted by the crush of the pedestrian flow, you commonly find yourself unable to safely deviate left or right and end up two suburbs away from your intended destination. Or, tripping over the gutter and finding yourself face down in the path of the oncoming, couldn't-give-a-shit, traffic.

A small amount of order and regimentation out

there, please. A touch of uniformity won't render us zombie-like, at least, no more than we already are.

At least we'll all avoid having to combine an innocent shopping experience with attendance at the emergency department of the local hospital.

SCORE = 89

By the way, as someone who includes being tragically anal on his CV, I also insist on walking on the left-hand side of the actual road. A massive over-reach you might say.

Too bad. Again, that's how I roll.

8.
WHAT THE HELL IS A 'LIFE COACH'?

8. WHAT THE HELL IS A 'LIFE COACH'?

'Life coach', 'social commentator', 'relationship coach', 'popular culture critic'? Really? Who *ARE* these people? Why are they here? Why do they harass and annoy us so incessantly? And, why don't they just go back to where they came from?

I suspect that some gifted individuals may hang up a shingle that proudly announces to the world their expertise in all such 'disciplines'. To accommodate a must-have, multi-career fallback approach to life. All these so-called 'qualifications' could very well have been obtained at the one time, fast-tracked and shrink-wrapped from the same, lesser-credentialed, bottom of a cornflakes box, tertiary 'educational institution' – with a complimentary graduate diploma in crystal healing thrown in for good measure.

My initial problem in taking the life coach concept seriously, or even getting close, is that I'm not altogether clear what a life coach actually does.

I've heard it said (in truth I cheated and Googled it again) that a life coach is a person 'who helps people take the "life journey" and guides them through the learnings they need in order to keep moving forward, stay on track and achieve success and happiness'.

In other words, a parent.

The bonus attached to the far less sexy Mum-and-Dad alternative is that the oldies are infinitely less expensive, allow you to sleep over, and occasionally feed you. (Never lose sight of the fact that their place is, unquestionably, the best hotel in town.)

Hot Tip: As a further life coach alternative, just take some time out to have a good old fashioned and honest chat to yourself. Jettison all the outside noise and talk to yourself 'straight'. Venture to somewhere quiet like a deserted beach or forest. Take your time – maybe a weekend. Do lots of deep breathing and throw in a dash of mindfulness. Forget the temptation of a wellness retreat, though. You're certain to bump into more life coaches than you can poke a stick at.

You'll work it out for yourself, cheaply, I promise, without the need for any amateur-professional external intervention.

If you're *still* stuck after that touch of priceless self-help, give me a call. I'll organise a 'pop-up' life coach for you. Mates rates, plus cab charge.

SCORE = 90

9.
CROWDS: TWO PEOPLE, INCLUDING ME

> *'Hell is other people'*
> — Jean-Paul Sartre

With few exceptions, I avoid crowds whenever I can, mainly because they unfailingly comprise people and noise, neither of which I'm terribly thrilled about.

I have the strong urge to not be wherever a crowd is. I rarely mix comfortably in any kind of gathering, feeling equally ill at ease (almost hyper-allergenic) in most social or professional environments. Even large family events, the theatre, groups of conference participants, restaurant diners, party goers, footy fans, drinking groups, or just a random bunch of work mates.

A crowd to me is two people, one of whom includes me.

Painfully shy, socially backward, put any tag on it that suits; the bottom line is: I missed my calling. The guy representing the Lighthouse Keepers Association of Australia failed to turn up on school 'careers night' when I was desperate for professional guidance. He was probably a deliberate no-show because of the potential crowd.

For me, a crowd is a jarring, debilitating and health-threatening shock to the senses that I can well do without, and generally do. Social distancing? Personal space enhancement? No problems. Bring it on!

Misanthropes of the world unite! I think I'll have T-shirts made.

9. CROWDS: TWO PEOPLE, INCLUDING ME

And crowdfund the cost.

SCORE = 96 (AND CLIMBING IMPERCEPTIBLY WITH EACH ADDITIONAL HEART PALPITATION)

10.
SNAKES

10. SNAKES

I don't like snakes and, quite frankly, couldn't give a stuff what they think of me.

I can't see the point. What's their purpose? Who invited them in the first place?

I'm not at all reluctant to admit that snakes, along with pissing me off monumentally, scare the living bejesus out of me. I'd very much prefer to live in a snake-less world but that's never going to happen unless I move to somewhere like Ireland or New Zealand.

That's never going to happen either. (Aside from practical reasons, like Covid, I'm convinced that neither country would have me – I wouldn't pass the character test, or a sanity check, or a sanitary check.)

In early October 2008, Mrs B and I were living blissfully as husband and wife (grump and grumpette) in Venus Bay, Victoria, when we unwittingly bumped into a local in the form of a tiger snake that had casually popped into the backyard to say 'cheers' and wish us well for the future.

Truth be told, it was our 130kg New Zealand house painter who spotted the snake, at or about the same time as the snake spotted him. They were equally unimpressed with each other. So they should've been, though the snake more so.

The snake bolted under the house, if snakes can bolt. Our brave, beefy Kiwi painter took off in the opposite direction, flying down the side fence-line like an All Black winger heading for the try line, before hurdling the front gate, diving into his truck head first, and disappearing into the distance at 150 clicks. He didn't return. He didn't send a bill for the half-painted house which, incidentally, he'd painted all black.

Needless to say, we were a tad spooked by this guy dropping in uninvited just to say hi (the snake, that is, not the boofy Kiwi) and sought some local advice. It was suggested that we purchase a device that's buried spike first in the ground and emits 'good vibrations' sending would-be intruders hither and slither.

We stationed four around the house at strategic locations. I insisted on installing 40, but Mrs B refused, somehow convincing me (she's good at that, after decades of practice) that the number I had in mind was a mild overreaction. From then on, whenever I ventured into the garden, a rare occurrence indeed, I made sure that I strapped at least one of these contraptions to my chest, and wore full-length gumboots and other assorted pieces of PPE. At which point, I looked remarkably like a fully kitted-out Ghostbuster.

The male version, not the newer, much-improved female model.

SCORE = 90

11.
RADIO SHOCK JOCKS: A WASTE OF VALUABLE OXYGEN

I guess the thing that pisses me off most about these guys is how inherently talentless they are. And, they're not confined to the radio either. Jocks and jockettes flourish shockingly on TV too.

Is it really such a tough gig? *Really*? Or is it just me? Let's be honest, surely the only 'skill' needed, based on how they *actually* conduct themselves, is being inventive enough to dream up different ways to be:

- *Rude*
- *Patronising*
- *Abusive*
- *Arrogant*
- *Dismissive*
- *Opinionated*
- *Obnoxious*
- *Ill-informed*
- *Shallow*
- *Inciteful*
- *Aggressive*
- *Self-important*
- *A dickhead*
- *Or, for the truly multi-talented, several of the above exhibited at roughly the same time*

As a society, can't we do better? What makes these people so special or worthy of our attention? Why do we feel compelled to tune in? Is it simply that we can't resist the temptation to feel sanctimonious and outraged?

In any case, it's rarely a two-way conversation, is it? Don't these people merely preach or invite us to agree with *them*? Of course, ratings must play a huge part, even if they're shrinking fast or weren't all that high in the first place.

Though relatively small in numbers, shock jocks/jockettes seem to pack a disproportionately powerful punch. They certainly manage to scare the tripe out of a sizeable bunch of weak-kneed, bootlicking, knee-jerking politicians. And, of course, members of this fraternity *have* been known to play their part in bringing down democratically chosen prime ministers, so there must be a misplaced 'talent' factor there, somewhere.

It's just that I can't see it.

Their only saving grace for me is that they appear to be perpetually grumpy. Or is it just contrived outrage (combined nevertheless with natural, ingrained malevolence) designed to maintain an ever-shrinking audience?

Or are they simply just a rag-tag bunch of fake grumps who, cynically, are merely 'in it for a quid' and desperate to be re-contracted next year?

In the interest of fair-mindedness, not to mention human decency, how about we all do ourselves a huge favour and simply stop listening to these people? Let's deprive them of the oxygen they need to survive, in the belief that one day, they'll be remembered – as they should be – as puffed up, rancorous, out-of-touch, but thankfully extinct relics of a bygone era.

Stuffed, shoved behind a glass case, hidden in the dusty basement of a rundown museum and wheeled out once a year, and only once a year, to remind us: were people ever *that* daft, or blatantly hoodwinked into listening to them in the first place?

SCORE = 95

12.
PEOPLE-SPREADERS

I'm very conscious of another person's physical space, mainly because of my somewhat neurotic need to protect my own.

When it comes to personal space, I have a strict and rigid policy to never usurp, encroach, impose, bump, touch, tickle, annex, invade, declare war, fire off scud missiles or otherwise cross territorial borders. Physically, I keep very much to myself and encourage others to do the same. I travel everywhere with my own portable force field. An invisible layer of bubble wrap. My own personal no man's land. My no-go zone.

I don't spread my legs at a forty-five-degree angle (a physiological impossibility for me anyway) and always tuck my arms in when seated in a row of seats. A strong and deeply felt suggestion to all airlines: please introduce an arm rest dotted-line policy on all your planes. Simply dash off a series of dotted lines down the exact centre of each arm rest to delineate the point past which it is forbidden, by law, to stray. This should eliminate any and all disputes as to where personal boundaries start and finish. No wonder I go to great lengths to always reserve an aisle seat. It automatically cuts the invasion factor down by fifty per cent. That's a good stat for a nut job like me.

You'll understand, then, why I'm no fan of open-plan offices. To me, they merely encourage outrageous and flagrant attempts at desk-space domination or outright bench-top territorial overthrow.

By the way, what's with these new-fangled pop-up

12. PEOPLE-SPREADERS

workstations that rise, with the press of a button, pulpit-like from the conventional tummy-level? I've sat at one in the past, but I've been too chicken-shit to press the 'up' arrow, fearing that it'll become locked at chin level, or just keep heading north, wiping out the ceiling above. I don't 'engage' successfully with mechanical devices, as you know.

My unbelievably brilliant daughter, Jess (I'm using 'brilliant' in its true sense here and not as a bullshit buzzword) has suggested that the hugely annoying practice of 'man-spreading' warranted a separate entry in the Top 100 List.

While I get where she's coming from and don't disagree in the slightest (a good career move in the case of my darling daughter), I don't believe it's inappropriate to attribute this dreadful habit to *both* sexes.

The spreading of the legs by the bullfrog male, whether on planes, trains, automobiles or anywhere in between, is a gross, disturbing and wholly selfish act. No argument there from me.

But, in my experience, the female of the species is no less guilty of encroaching on other people's space. Next time you're out and about at, say, a bank, a supermarket or other public place where there's even a micro-centimetre of unused bench or table space, watch in shock and awe, and outright horror, at what gets hauled out of, and paraded from, the personal shipping container that is … **THE WOMAN'S HANDBAG.**

This deserves its own entry in the Top 100 List, and it shall have it.

Read on.

SCORE = 92

13.
THE MINDLESS PREOCCUPATION WITH MOBILE PHONES

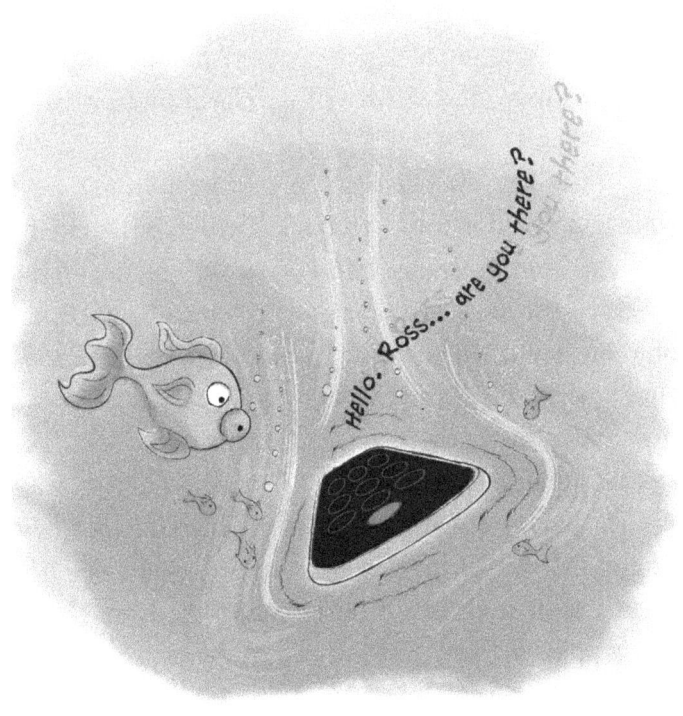

I accept that I may get some grudging acknowledgement, but very little agreement, let alone traction, on this one.

The addiction has well and truly taken hold and, now that it's in pandemic dimensions, there's no cure and there's no going back. It's mobile world out there and I've been left far, far behind. And, I must say, I feel a great sense of joy in admitting it. Bordering on happiness.

I have to confess that phones of any description annoy the crap out of me (maybe I'll cover my crazy phone phobia in Volume Two), but much more so does the obsession with the mobile variety.

The mere sound of a 'personalised' mobile ring tone sends me into orbit. Such self-indulgent and intrusive nonsense.

I turn my mobile on only spasmodically, and whingeingly. I don't 'do' Facebook, Twitter, Instagram or Snapchat, and I wouldn't know an app if it bit me on the arse. I've also resisted the urge to download 729 iTunes onto my device. In any case, I wouldn't have the faintest clue how to. I'll never run the risk of needing to have my mobile surgically removed. And, at last count, I've 'texted' (is there such a word?) five times in my life.

The pervasive instant-ness of the mobile is a source of blind terror for me. I simply do not want to be *that* accessible or reachable. I can't afford to be from a well-being point of view. Just ask any of those three people who know me what my views are about the spur of the moment mobile-initiated 'catch up'.

13. THE MINDLESS PREOCCUPATION WITH MOBILE PHONES

For me, the mobile is a last-resort means of communication, nothing more, and especially not to be used as a toy or a source of entertainment.

If I had my way (never likely), I'd trek back to Sydney where I grew up (even by plane with Boofheads 1 and 2 in tow), pay to do the Harbour Bridge Climb (and endure the trauma of a mini-crowd experience) and, as a wonderfully symbolic, middle-fingered act of defiance and complete disdain for technology, would take great joy in hurling my mobile into the Harbour – *never* to be replaced. Thereafter, when asked the inevitable question: 'Where's your mobile?' I'd have undeniable joy in replying: 'It sleeps with the fishes'.

Now, *that's* empowerment!

I have not, in any sense, embraced technology (no kidding?) and have absolutely no inclination or need to. Let me give you an example, and one that I'm exceedingly chuffed to recount.

I was recently requested to take a photo of a certain emailed document with my mobile and then send the signed version to another mobile number 'via MMS'. To counter such lunacy, I did the only sensible thing a person of my technological ineptitude would do: I copied the document onto a USB stick. I then drove some distance to the nearest library and printed the document out. I then drove back home to have Mrs B sign the document. Next, I drove back to the library and scanned the signed document back onto the USB. I then completed this simple task by driving home again and emailing the signed document back to the person who had the temerity to demand that I do it her way. The whole bizarre exercise took over four hours to complete and cost about $50 in petrol.

Even more recently, I was requested to 'copy the link and place it onto Microsoft Edge'. This means jack to me and I care about it even less.

Get stuffed technology. You're not going to push *me* around!

I once worked on a gas plant construction site 40km outside of Darwin where, as we approached the gas 'commissioning' stage, all mobile phones (and other electronic devices) were banned. The result, in this day and age, was nothing less than revolutionary. Except for those who quit because they simply couldn't go without their devices (and this was a decent percentage of the work force, mind you), the ban had breathtaking social consequences. On lunch breaks and 'smoko' – actual smoking had, understandably, also been banned some months earlier – and on the otherwise tedious hour-long bus commute to and from Darwin, people resorted to the strangest practices to while away the time. They played chess, read books, knitted, wrote, studied and, would you believe, actually engaged in conversation (except me, of course).

Btw (my favourite trendy buzzword abbreviation), *must* you take a shot of this morning's baked beans on

13. THE MINDLESS PREOCCUPATION WITH MOBILE PHONES

toast and post it on Facebook? Is that so Earth-shatteringly important to the rest of the universe?

And Selfies? Well, we'll come to that plainly obnoxious behaviour later. It easily warrants its own separate entry.

And, so it shall have it, but only in a manner of speaking.

SCORE = 97 – NO, STUFF IT, LET'S NOT DICK AROUND ON THIS ONE: **100**

14.
SHIT HAPPENINGS

14. SHIT HAPPENINGS

It'll come as no surprise to learn that I became intimately acquainted with the 'shit happens' principle at a very early age.

We've kept in close contact ever since and have developed a grudging acceptance of each other, though never a lasting friendship. It's not that I'm reckless or live life on the edge – far from it. At best/worst, I'm a closet non-conformist. But shit nevertheless just seems to happen and follows me and sticks to me wherever I venture.

Not earth-moving truckloads of the stuff, just small, irritating, pellet-size nuggets that get flicked at me when I'm not paying attention and drop my guard. Like spit balls catapulted at you in the school classroom. Sometimes, though, the principle gets pushed well beyond a tolerable level. We'll come to that.

I'd much prefer to be the shit-*er* but am, more consistently, the shit-*ee*. It's certainly not always been that way, but often enough to convince me that life, generally, 'is what it is'.

I've never seen the glass as being half full or half empty. For me, it's just half a glass. No more, no less.

The shit happens/'it is what it is' principle has, ever since I can remember, been the filter through which I tend to view life and the world.

Playing your hand as best you can, with the cards you're dealt: acceptance and acknowledgement, but not capitulation by any means.

There's a world of difference.

SCORE = 70

The relatively low score reflects my strong belief that the shit happens principle is simply a fact of life to be recognised, and negotiated and dealt with, along with chronically bad doses of diarrhoea which are, let's face it, the logical and conspicuous consequences of the shit happens principle in any case.

15.
HAVING TO BEND DOWN AND TOUCH MY TOES

Sorry guys, I simply can't do it.

Not even if I spread my legs, which I can't manage either with any degree of success without running the risk of ripping a hammy. I can barely make it past the top of my shin bone. Certainly not mid-shin, no way. This means that slip-on shoes are a must and socks suck.

To put it plainly and bluntly, I have the suppleness and flexibility of a bowling ball.

And the good looks and sparkling personality, to match.

Consequently, I have absolutely no idea what's going on that far south. I can only observe my toes from afar (with the aid of high-powered binoculars and/or GPS) and hope like hell that if a disaster strikes (such as growing a sixth digit, or a root vegetable anywhere between digits one to five), some kind soul will give me a heads up.

That endgame suits me, though, as I find that part of the body, especially mine, not remotely interesting, let alone fascinating or worthy of any regular scrutiny.

From time to time I'm obliged to examine, monkey-like, Mrs B's toe region. Whilst that exercise doesn't piss me off (much), it's nevertheless shockingly disturbing, as the good Mrs B's feet and all 11.5 toes have for some considerable time now been more Hobbit-like than human.

At least she's good for a spud or two, and the odd grossly deformed carrot.

SCORE = 86

16.
HERNIAS AND THE UNWANTED DUCK EGG

While on the subject of physical misfortune …

Physios love me, and I swear I can see the dollar signs light up in their eyes whenever I crawl crab-like into their consultation rooms.

The same goes for dermatologists (the many visits to whom are the unplanned by-products of a misspent youth on Sydney beaches) and, as I was to discover more recently, surgeons.

In extremely graphic detail, the surgeon in question – I think this boy had just flown in from Brazil – explained to me (and the medically savvy Mrs B, who was in her element and foaming at the mouth in anticipation) how he was going to slice and dice me to repair, as a mechanic would repair a punctured tyre, my increasingly bulging right groin. By then, it was about the size and shape of a duck egg. 'For that matter,' he added, 'why don't I do the left-hand side at the same time', as it was bound to 'go' sometime in the future anyway?

It was on the tip of my tongue to enquire whether this two-for-the-price-of-one special deal came with fries, a set of steak knives or a family-size bucket of KFC. I stopped short, though, anxious not to upset the very person who, soon enough, would be hovering above me with scalpel in hand as I lay comatose on the operating table, ready to 'do me' like a side of beef in an abattoir.

Mrs B would've booked ringside seats for the gloriously gory show if she could've.

So, there it was. If I chose to, I could carry on through

16. HERNIAS AND THE UNWANTED DUCK EGG

life with the blissful knowledge that I'd magically grown a lump in my groin so big that I bore a striking resemblance to the Three-Testicled Lady in the circus.

Coincidentally, at or about the same time, I was suffering with a lower back so stiff that I could barely manage the turning circle of the Titanic.

Otherwise OK?

SCORE = 85

P.S. The groin op. was a resounding success and these days, possessing one less duck egg to cart around, and being decidedly lighter, I no longer in any way resemble a testicular version of the Elephant Man. The uncooperative lower back persists, however, along with rat-shit Achilles tendons and other assorted biomechanical irregularities.

17.
OSTENTATIOUS WEDDINGS: WHY DO WE BOTHER?

17 OSTENTATIOUS WEDDINGS: WHY DO WE BOTHER?

And when I say 'ostentatious', I mean virtually any modern-day wedding at all.

When the good Mrs B surprisingly agreed to tie the knot back in 1977 (don't forget, this was the era of the psychedelic mushroom), celebrations of marriage were simple and relaxed – due, at least in part, to wonderful batches of those psychedelic mushrooms. Our wedding ceremony was held in the front yard of her parent's home in East Lindfield, Sydney, and the reception was held in the backyard. Consequently, there was no need for a fleet of limos to ferry us about. No hostilities were waged over the pruning of the guest list. Rather, we were flat out thinking of people to invite, especially on my side, for obvious reasons. There was no printed, gold-embossed order of service, which, in truth, we made up as we went along. And, there was no twenty-person wedding party that closely resembles the TV commentary team on election night, and no need to arrange valet parking.

The wedding was very low-key by today's ludicrously extravagant benchmark. There was no fancy wedding ceremony 'space', no lavish $200-a-head 'do' afterwards in some tasteless Taj Mahal-like reception venue, no rehearsals or practice makeovers, and not a beach or a forest in sight. And, thankfully, our wedding was well before '*You Are The Wind Beneath My Wings*' (or the Adele/Beyoncé/Taylor Swift equivalent) had become a compulsory part of the marriage service.

On the other hand, the wedding wasn't exactly

Dimboola-like either. There were no blues, punch-ups or hissy fits. No tears were shed in anger, and the police weren't called to break up warring factions – family, religious, ethnic, or otherwise. It was just a very simple celebration which we both thoroughly enjoyed and have had fond memories of ever since.

Neither did it cost my father-in-law, Colin, the equivalent of the GDP of a developing country, or the contents of Malcolm Turnbull's spare change jar. Nor did it delay his retirement by ten years either – Col's not Malc's, that is.

Come to think of it, we actually enjoyed the wedding we really wanted. How many newlyweds can truly make that claim?

C'mon guys. Is it really worth the drama, stress and humungous expense? Go easy. Go minimalist. Go without. Make a donation to your favourite charity instead.

Or just elope.

Or just don't bother.

SCORE = 92

P.S. Not sure whether Harry and Megs would agree, or Will and Kate for that matter.

By the way, my laid-back marriage proposal to the up-for-it Mrs B was neither grossly public and captured on camera just in time for the seven o'clock news, nor very romantic. From memory (though, I admit, that's not an accurate guide by any means), it was more along the lines of: 'Got much on this Saturday arvo?'

18.
CANBERRA BASHING AND WHAT IT MEANS FOR ULAANBAATAR

18. CANBERRA BASHING

Don't you reckon it's a bit stiff that Canberra bashing continues to be a time-honoured and popular sport amongst many Australians? 'No,' I hear you say. Well too bad. It's my book and I'll make the point anyway.

To me at least, Canberra and Canberrans often appear to be on the receiving end even if you've developed a troublesome hemorrhoid condition or your footy team happened to have lost on the weekend. (My theory is that the recently-arrived cane toads were deliberately introduced into the national capital by a particularly pissed off individual – not me this time – who didn't appreciate his latest tax bill, or her latest Prime Ministerial offering.)

I was once, way back in 1982, on the wrong end of a spray in Brisbane for being from 'Cambra' (I was sporting an ACT singlet at the time), and that was at the 35km mark of a marathon. I'd just lurched past a group of spectators, one of whom, with palpable hostility, declared:

'*Here comes Malcolm bloody Fraser. Boo!!*'

As I'd long been a 'true believer' and had witnessed the sacking of the Whitlam Government first-hand in 1975 while a student at the ANU, the below-the-belt comment was especially galling. Even if I'd wanted to, I was too stuffed to respond and just meekly shuffled past without so much as a two fingered salute. I would've gladly settled for giving them the bird, but couldn't raise the energy to lift my arm, or even the middle finger that it required.

It's rarely the government that incurs the wrath, and it actually *sits* in Canberra (if only spasmodically, some would argue), but curiously, Canberra itself. It's as if Canberrans get together at a Happy Hour on a Friday afternoon every week, have a few drinks, get smashed and, in group-think fashion, collectively make decisions that are deliberately designed to stuff the rest of us.

I suggest we pinched the practice from the Yanks, who heap considerable venom on the many diabolical things that 'Washington' inflicts on US citizens on a regular basis. I'm not sure if the same kind of finger pointing is ever directed at Minsk, Mogadishu or Ulaanbaatar.

Leave the good folk of Canberra alone, I say. Though you may occasionally lose sight of this fact, they're Australians too. A Canberran is as Australian as a Queensland coal miner, a FIFO worker from WA, a wine grower from the Barossa Valley, or a potato farmer from Tassie.

Forget all the 'Canberra bubble' bunkum. That's just a convenient, but rubbish, excuse promoted by self-serving, bubble-headed politicians of the Prime Ministerial kind. And, forget what actually goes on in Parliament House, too.

Besides, our national capital cousins are the *only* people in the country who *truly* understand the road rules for roundabouts.

SCORE = 91

19.
TIPTOEING THROUGH THE TULIPS: POLITICAL CORRECTNESS GONE BERSERK

I have to be careful here. Maybe, even politically correct. (Very unlikely.)

On the one hand, I'm a great believer in freedom of speech with a few, but clearly defined, boundaries. Mind you, I'm not smart enough to know where those boundaries should be drawn. On the other hand, I know words *can* and *do* hurt.

Although I'm genuinely mindful of the feelings of others (you don't have to like people to be courteous and respectful), I do get the strong impression that we're gradually sliding deeper into a childishly over-PC'd world. When, for instance, the suggestion is seriously entertained that we consider changing the name of Eggs and Bacon Bay because it's potentially offensive to the 'animal welfare' of chooks and pigs, or alternatively to our vegetarian brethren, well, words fail me.

It seems to me that our feelings are hurt far too easily these days. We're too afraid to speak out for fear of causing offence or giving rise to an action before one or more of the several anti-discrimination tribunals that have been established out there to protect the most vulnerable.

As a consequence, don't you think our words have become *too* well chosen? We skirt and tiptoe around topics or, to play it completely safe, avoid them altogether. We speak from autocues, talking points, and briefing notes. We stick to script and are schooled by minders to never deviate. When put on the spot and forced to improvise, we shut the interview down and hurriedly move on.

19. TIPTOEING THROUGH THE TULIPS

We've lost the art of shooting from the hip, of telling it like it is, of calling a spade a spade – or we're heavily reprimanded and derided when we do. Even our so-called ad-lib moments appear well rehearsed. Our off-the-cuff responses are deeply choreographed and plucked automatically from our mental Rolodex. Authenticity has been replaced by spin, image and hidden agendas.

The very best public speaking, for instance, used to be about telling your story, raw, unedited and from the heart. You'd hear it on a soapbox in The Domain in Sydney. Now, an eloquently delivered but sterile speech, meticulously prepared by a gaggle of professional speech writers, is, as a telling insight into where we've now arrived, sadly applauded as a 'polished performance'.

On another level, many people seem to exist nowadays, and even thrive, in a world of perpetual moral outrage. Being perpetually offended has become fashionable, and a commodity ripe for exploitation. As a result, the crusader (boosted by a book launch, national speaking tour, marketing manager and a newly appointed life coach), has become infinitely more important than the cause. Next professional career move: 'celebrity social commentator'.

Maybe I'm being a touch cynical (who, me?) but I fully expect there are people out there, somewhere, actually profiting from the commercialisation of outrage. An 'industry', no doubt, that will soon require tariff protection, government grant or a pork barrelling sports rort.

Anyway, back to the point. Why should we feel so mortally wounded by:
- *Manholes? ('maintenance holes')*
- *Easter eggs? ('spring spheres')*
- *Brainstorming? ('thought showers')*
- *Jolly Santa's 'ho, ho, ho'? (apparently, there's no PC alternative)*
- *Christmas trees? ('holiday trees')*
- *Expectant mothers? ('pregnant people')*

Yes, they're words. Just words. How do they hurt or insult? Surely, they're not even flesh wounds. When they lack malicious intent, how do they slice through and denigrate in a meaningful or lasting way? They were acceptable then, relevant to the time and regarded as inoffensive. Why have they become *so* unacceptable now?

Have we nothing better to do, nothing profoundly more important (like seriously addressing climate change [and not merely paying lip service to it], sensible water management, disability care, domestic violence, mental health issues, child obesity, etc.) than to spend vast quantities of valuable human energy and intellect on such trivial pursuits? How much better is the community served by a preoccupation with the breathtakingly insignificant?

Being sensitive, and acting appropriately, with respect to the feelings of others is one thing. Being too afraid to open your mouth for fear of sticking your foot in it is

19. TIPTOEING THROUGH THE TULIPS

another thing altogether. Obviously, I'm not intelligent enough to make an informed choice between the two.

But, aren't most of us mature enough to tell the difference? Can't we inject our reasonableness, judgment and sense of balance, and simply walk away or self-censor if we find something objectionable? Do our sensibilities need to be *so* protected?

Or is it just *me*?

SCORE = 93

P.S. '*I disapprove of what you say, but I'll defend to the death your right to say it.*'

– Evelyn Beatrice Hall

20.
UNSUCCESSFULLY EATING A PIE WHILE DRIVING

20. UNSUCCESSFULLY EATING A PIE WHILE DRIVING

Yeah, OK, I can guess what you're thinking here. How irresponsible and unsafe of me to attempt such a ridiculous feat, let alone attempt to glorify the practice, blah, blah, blah!

Regardless of this well-founded criticism, I've attempted the forlorn task many times in the past and, no doubt, will continue to do so despite the same Ground Hog Day catastrophe.

It goes something like this:

- *My first big mistake is to take the first bite. Once the tongue engages with the lava-like contents of the pie (meat, chicken or whatever), the brain relays the awful truth (which I already knew but chose to ignore) that the pie filling is way too volcanic for human consumption.*
- *The inevitable end result of this brain/tongue miscommunication (apart from the burnt tongue which I'll still have a week later) is to deposit the steaming contents of my mouth somewhere downstairs in the nether region of my crotch (and onto my newly dry-cleaned pants), after it has first stumbled, fumbled and rolled its way downwards over my once pristine white shirt.*
- *The next big mistake is to place the pie on the middle console to cool – within easy sniffing, licking and nibbling distance of my furry, four-legged friend who's been lurking silently in the back seat waiting patiently for me to repeat the same daft act*

- *I've performed on at least 347 previous occasions.*
- *Once my brain clicks back into gear, about two hours later, and reminds me that the pie is now (or was an hour ago) relatively edible, I reach down and grab it, or what's left of it after my back-seat passenger has had his turn.*
- *On my second bite, my brain tells me two things. Firstly, that the once scalding contents of the pie are now stone cold. Secondly, that much of the delicious pie contents have been replaced by not-so-delicious dog hair and dog slobber.*
- *The inevitable end result of the second bite is to repeat the outcome of the first.*
- *By this time, my shirt and pants resemble a patchwork quilt of pie filling, gravy and crumbs (as well as dog hair/drool), a substantial clump of which has now congealed down in that crotchy nether region, hence welding my bum stickily to the car seat.*
- *Of course, I'm then forced to stop at the next servo to clean up … and buy another pie to replace the one I didn't get to eat the first time around. And, buy a sausage roll for the dog to keep him happy … and take his mind off the new p*ie.

SCORE = 89

21.
BABY GIRLS' FLORAL HEADBANDS: THE PARENTAL TRIBUTE

Is the now compulsory baby girls' floral headband supposed to make the baby look cute or is it just a 'look-how-clever-we-are' moment for Mum and Dad?

In reality, it looks absurd. It's right up there with the wearing of baseball caps back-to-front, and animals dressed up as human beings. What a total insult to animals that is.

It's a *baby*. It doesn't need, much less deserve, to be dressed up like a Christmas tree. It's smiling because it's just passed wind, not because it's overjoyed at the silly floral pompom that dopy Mum or Dad has plonked on its forehead.

It's a *baby*, not a (floral) tribute to the parents. (Despite what you mistakenly think, you're *NOT* the only people on the planet clever enough to have given birth.)

It's a *baby*, there's no hiding the stark reality that the kid has no hair.

It's a *baby*, not a showpiece or a circus act.

It's a *baby*, not a parental adornment or living, breathing appendage, or fashion accessory that you bung in your handbag/manbag.

Give the kid a break. Cut it some slack. It'll become traumatised soon enough by the ravages of life, and by being baby-shamed on social media, without being forced into the process prematurely by unthinking, attention-seeking bozo parents.

SCORE = 93

22.
TAJ MAHAL-STYLE McMANSIONS

Early in 1978, Mrs B and I took the plunge and bought our first house.

It was located out in the Canberra burbs, in the only area we could afford at the time. In truth, my awesome sister Sheila (the genuine kind, not the shallow buzzword version) found the house for us at 15 Yarra Street, Kaleen. The house, a cute salt-and-pepper-coloured brick butter box, was for sale for $34,950. (Yes, that was the full sale price, not just the five per cent deposit.)

We paid the deposit by credit card (don't try this at home kids) and took out two mortgages. We weren't consciously part of any 'we want it all and we want it now' movement. That state of being would come later with an enhanced level of maturity and sophistication. We were just desperate to set up house together, as most newly married couples are.

We lived for many months with a double bed – we thought that was very special after our single-bed 'graduate house' student accommodation days – and nothing much else. Our fridge for the first several months was a leaky, second-hand esky and we had no washing machine, let alone a dishwasher or microwave.

The house was definitely no energy-sucking McMansion. It actually *had* a backyard (standard issue in those days) and didn't occupy an entire but miniscule block. A remarkable and pleasing side-benefit of this was that you couldn't hear your next-door neighbour gargle, or fart.

The house had no games room, lap pool, gym, study,

pool-side cabana, rooftop garden, vertical wall garden, media room, reading nook, internal lift for the second storey, or ensuites to all eight bedrooms (or, the late 1970s equivalents). Nor did we have an outdoor entertainment area, a spa, a true-blue Aussie/Balinese gazebo, or a touch of Mediterranean or Scandinavian ambience in the backyard.

Our idea of al fresco living was sitting on the back patio (in fact, just a concrete slab) with a primitive BBQ made by stacking a few bricks left over from the building of the house, and which I didn't even 'glue' together. Guess what? It cooked snags and chops (obviously this was well before the vegan, gluten free, organically grown, barbecued eggplant days). It did the job.

Regrettably, these days, due partly to poor planning, greedy developers and rate-seeking local councils, the everyday, contemporary urban landscape has been well and truly over-cooked. The cheek-by-jowl approach to new housing development commonly results in aesthetically unappealing urban wastelands and (sorry, Kevin) only a tiny number of truly 'grand designs' and certainly no 'house of the year' offerings.

I find this truly sad, shocking and shameful.

SCORE = 94

23.
SPEED BUMPS AND BROKEN TEETH

23. SPEED BUMPS AND BROKEN TEETH

I don't have the stats on it but, holy crap, they're exceedingly annoying, particularly when located in places where they surely don't need to be. Like carparks.

And, why are they so often the height, shape and configuration of Mount Everest? In some instances they're so high that halfway into their negotiation, your vehicle becomes immovably marooned on top of the speed bump with all four wheels spinning like the clappers but producing a tractionless, motionless, jack-shit response. Whereupon, the vehicle then has to be airlifted out and taken to the nearest wrecking yard because its undercarriage has been scraped, crunched and flogged well beyond repair.

Not to mention the fact that in the process of jarringly bashing into the north face of Everest, you've lost three of your front teeth and several back fillings.

Send the bills, vehicle, dental and otherwise, to the local council, which'll be only too pleased to cough up and pay for all expenses incurred.

Yeah, that'll happen.

SCORE = 87

24.
SMALL CHILDREN (AND LARGER ONES TOO)

24. SMALL CHILDREN

It won't come as much of a surprise to learn that I'm not hugely fond of children.

And that has nothing to do with the fact that I'm grandchild-less. This is a state of being with which, I can assure you, I'm exceedingly relaxed and comfortable. In any case, I'd make a crap grandad by all accounts, especially mine.

Their much-touted cuteness (kids, not grandads) is lost on me I'm afraid. Am I mistaken in thinking that it's readily accepted nowadays that we should all be overjoyed to be living in a dummy-less world? Or, am I just like I am with most modern-day phenomena, way behind the times?

When it comes to plane travel (about which, as you know, I have very ordinary feelings), I reckon dummies (OK, use the buzzword 'child pacifiers' if you must) should be handed out with headsets as standard issue. And preferably, automatically plugged into the kid's gob as it's marched, wheeled or otherwise escorted on board. (Maybe, a couple for Mum and Dad, too?)

In April 2017, I travelled to Boston to run the Boston Marathon, four days after my 65th birthday. I was a trifle pissed at being forced, at great personal inconvenience and expense, to travel to Boston to 'run Boston', but what the heck. Perspective, again.

On flight QF 0093 (Melbourne to Los Angeles), we were blessed with a veritable smorgasbord of squawking toddlers. I hesitate to use the word 'brats' as, generally speaking, I accept that they know not what they do. Except for one little treasure who knew exactly what she was doing when she swiped my muffin in the course of one of the many laps she made around the cabin as if she were training for the mini marathon at the next Grots Olympics. Her name was probably something trendy and obnoxious, like Apple. Or maybe that was her middle name, the first name being even more objectionable, like Custard. Or Stewed. Or Peeled. Or, most fittingly, Rotten.

Of course, the mother laughingly dismissed this random and deliberate kamikaze attack as just another example of baby gorgeousness. I didn't see the funny side – no surprises there – even less so after we'd prised the helpless bakery treat from the kid's mitt (finger by finger), by which time what was left of it had been reduced to a mangled mess, and was then promptly deposited into my mitt to eat if I dared. I *did* dare and shoved it straight down my throat right in front of the horror just to piss *her* off.

It must've done the trick, as she then let out a high-pitched wail (which, apparently, only the smallest child is physically capable of making) and high-tailed it back to dopey Mum, who stared incredulously at me as if I'd mentally scarred the kid, and her, for life. I wouldn't have been at all concerned if I had.

The old adage, 'children should be seen but not heard' is only partly true. They really should only be publicly displayed on the odd occasion, like Christmas and Easter,

24. SMALL CHILDREN

and then only for about 30 minutes each time. Or, in the opinion of the equally wonderfully child-intolerant Mrs B, small children should be removed to the middle of the Australian desert (I know just the place) and only permitted to return (with the almost-impossible-to-obtain, hard line, Dutton-inspired visa) when they've reached their mid-forties.

The International Year of the Child is alive and well, and has a lot to answer for!

SCORE = 97 (AND CLIMBING – THE PERFECT 100 IS WITHIN PLAIN SIGHT)

25.
BEER THAT'S LESS THAN ICY COLD (AND RELATED BOUTIQUE IRRITATIONS)

25. BEER THAT'S LESS THAN ICY COLD

It's a ritual from which it's impossible for me to escape. I'm simply compelled to take a beer from the fridge, no matter how cold it is already, and shove it in the freezer for at least 20 minutes before drinking it. Any beer that doesn't have flecks of ice floating in it is borderline tepid and undrinkable.

Most people, if they're pissed off fusspots like me, will send food back. Me, I send beer back unless it's gone through the freezer chilling process.

Equally irritating for me are the so-called craft or boutique beers. I don't give a flying you-know-what how trendy or 'now' the boutique beer industry is. Maybe I rail against it *because* of its 'boutique-ness'.

Regardless, even though I may be way out of step with conventional tastes (and loving it), I simply do not want a 'funky sour ale', a 'woodie malt', a 'sweet and roastie ale', a beer that has 'notes' of citrus, herbs, coffee and cream, cherry, raspberry or peach, or a beer that has 'flavours reminiscent of summer fruit salad' with a 'hint of cloves at the finish'. And, I can well do without the look of complete disdain and the rolling of the eyes from the dickhead waiter when I'm forced to settle for a lemon, lime and bitters following my forlorn search of the drinks menu for a beer that's remotely to my liking from the list of 125 on offer.

Like milk with the dollop, I just want a beer that tastes like real beer.

Otherwise, bugger off and bring me a chocolate malted milkshake.

SCORE = 91

26.
THE RELENTLESS QUEST FOR INSTANT NOW-NESS

Whadda we want?
Everything!
When do we want it?
Now!

In truth, 'now' is far too late for most people. 'Yesterday' only just qualifies as mildly acceptable. 'Last week' is really what we had in mind. Bizarrely, even history documentaries are now cast in the present tense to make them more contemporary and seemingly more believable or easier for us to understand. (More on that delight later. It can't escape unscathed or unscrutinised.)

Two-minute noodles seem to take an eternity to cook, even when they take only two minutes. The mere fact that we're required to cook them at all is exceptionally annoying as well. Such a waste of time. You'd think that *someone* could've at least invented the one-minute variety by now.

Most things these days must be instant, express, or otherwise fast-tracked. If it doesn't have an 'urgent' stamp on it, whack it on anyway just to make sure you're not forgotten or that you get a response well before you actually need it.

From the fifteen-minute news cycle to 20/20 cricket, we want it all and we want it now. Just add water, stir (it's a tedious chore and once is enough), microwave for thirty seconds and serve.

26. THE RELENTLESS QUEST FOR INSTANT NOW-NESS

Overnight sensation. Fast food (what the hell is a slow-cooked roast?). University degrees 'while-you-wait'. Exercise for five minutes a day and lose twenty kilos in two weeks (are you telling me I can't get the same result *without* the exercise?). Become 'instantly mindful' at a weekend wellness retreat (please 'make it happen' on Friday afternoon after work so I'll have the weekend free … and still be able to enjoy Friday night.)

Surely, there's no better example of our search for instant now-ness than the delivery of news. We demand to be immediately and fully informed. We examine *all* events – even the relatively trivial – forensically, microscopically and repetitively, aided by the ever-present panel of experts, many of whom, in fact, tell us little more than the blindingly obvious. Or spruik highly biased and dubious opinions that hide personal agendas.

Nevertheless, nothing gets by. Nothing slips through the net. We breathlessly await the next 'breaking news' event. The pace is frenetic, exhausting and addictive.

Do we really need to be *so* continually informed, *so* tuned in, *so* wired up and wired? Not me. I'd rather go bush and get off the grid, where 'they' can't get me, whoever 'they' are at any given time. And there's lots of 'them' out there, too.

For me, it's simply a question of being close enough to the things that matter and far enough away from the things that don't. If the world is about to come to a catastrophic end, surely someone will let me know, soon enough.

In any event, I'd scarcely bother to get out of the way.

SCORE = 90

27.
MISPRONOUNCED WORDS

Lackadaisical Camaraderie Vulnerable Prerogative Picture Excavation Mischievous Antarctic Triathlon Police Turmeric Vice versa Asterisk Regardless Probably Integral

Some notable examples:
- *Camaraderie (no, not comrarderie.)*
- *Vulnerable (the most mispronounced word in the English language. The word has an 'l' in it, between the 'u' and the 'n'! It's there for a purpose. I beg of you, please use it!)*
- *Antarctic (the word is quite happy as it is. It really doesn't need its first 'c' to be mysteriously deleted.)*
- *Triathlon (the word is quite happy as it is. It really doesn't need a second 'a' after the 'h'.)*
- *Police (there's an 'o' in there for very good reason.)*
- *Turmeric (don't forget the first 'r'.)*
- *Probably (don't forget the second 'b'.)*
- *Integral (the 'r' loves being where it is. It's not happy being relocated after the 't'.)*
- *Prerogative (it's 'rer' not just 'er'.)*
- *Lackadaisical (there's nothing 'lax' about this word.)*
- *Picture (the object this word is mistaken for holds water – mispronouncing 'picture' doesn't.)*
- *Excavation (yes, it really does have an 'x', not an 's'.)*
- *Regardless (irregardless of whether you think 'irregardless' is acceptable, believe me, it isn't and never will be.)*
- *Mischievous (it's quite comfortable with two 'i's. It really doesn't want a third.)*
- *Asterisk (here's a tip for you, this word doesn't like its 's' and 'k' to be reversed.)*

27. MISPRONUNCED WORDS

- *Vice versa (I just can't bring myself to talk about the longstanding abuse of this expression.)*

And, as a caring, considerate and cooperative society, can we please, when we speak, stop sounding words that end in 'd' as if they end in 't' – 'and', 'mind', 'world', 'Queensland', 'weekend', 'island' etc.

Time to take a deep breath, guys.

It takes no appreciable extra effort to pronounce words correctly than it does to get them wildly wrong. It just takes a little time, practice and maybe some serious teeth/tongue/brain thynchwonithashon.

SCORE = 92

28.
HAVING TO ENGAGE WITH THE COMMUNITY

28. HAVING TO ENGAGE WITH THE COMMUNITY

This'll come as a lightbulb moment of revelation – I simply don't.

As I've already mentioned, I tend to shy away from people as much as possible. Sad and concerning as this may appear to many, and definitely not 'normal' to most, I don't feel at all obliged to engage with the community. However, I *do* have an abiding respect for the individual rights and freedoms of others, and consciously practice it on a simple, everyday basis.

(As a quirky paradox, it amazes me how many people who proudly trumpet to the world that they 'love people', in fact, treat the very same people with total disrespect and contempt.)

To be clear, if a person needs help, I'll be there until 'it's all good'. I just won't turn up again tomorrow with a DJ's food hamper or a bowl of chicken soup. I'm unlikely to make a meal of it.

I don't crave social connection or interaction. Pandemic-driven or otherwise, self-isolation is never a problem for me. A people person I am not and I make no apologies for that. I don't regard it as a flaw in my character, though some do. You don't have to wear your heart on your sleeve to prove you have one. I'm *not* a miserable old coot. I just don't get invited to many parties. In any case, aren't we all seriously over-hugged and over-kissed as it is, even by complete strangers it seems, without me adding to it? (Why has the hug replaced the handshake?)

Unsurprisingly, I don't have a social circle, or even a

social semi-circle. In my case, it's more like a very short, straight line, possibly a dash or a hyphen, though not quite a full stop.

I also have no great desire to be included, let alone to join hands in a circle of people and chant *Kumbaya* or even hum along to *House of the Rising Sun*, for that matter. Just a small measure of grudging tolerance from you folks out there is good enough for me, as long as some kind soul is obliging enough to pass the salt or the tomato sauce, preferably without me having to ask for it.

It all reminds me of a famous quote from Groucho Marx:

> 'I sent the club a wire stating, "Please accept my resignation. I don't want to belong to any club that will accept me as a member."'

SCORE = 95 (AND CLIMBING - RAPIDLY)

29.
WHAT THE HELL IS A 'SOCIAL COMMENTATOR'?

The notion of what a 'social commentator' actually is, or is supposed to be, or pretends to be, perplexes me greatly, along similar lines to the 'life coach'.

And, I'm still trying to fathom how anyone could make a living from being a social commentator, as such, or why they even should. Their special subject is surely *'the bleeding obvious'*.

It's a vocation, or dare I say, a niche industry that we don't, in fact, need, created by those who've convinced us that we really do. It wouldn't be the first time that's happened. It's a bit like an overgrown HR department in a large organisation: existing and evolving for its own sake and sense of self-fulfilment, but performing no meaningful, practical function.

Surely, the same level of so-called informed social commentary can be obtained by having a few boofhead mates over for a Sunday arvo barbecue and talking absolute rubbish for a few hours – as you do – especially with a few grogs under your belt. But hopefully, you stop well short of running your brand new social theory through the Pub Test. I mean, how many intelligent national conversations have you ever had in a pub, especially after a few beers?

In any case, don't social commentators exist already in many and various forms? Aren't they called writers, poets, actors, songwriters, comedians, artists, musicians, public speakers (the old soap box variety, that is), hair-

29. WHAT THE HELL IS A 'SOCIAL COMMENTATOR'?

dressers, taxi drivers, and any dill who rants and raves on talkback radio?

If we need social commentators (as a special class of people with an official name tag and a title to give them credibility) to explain to us what we should already know, or what just happened, or otherwise to explain to us that we're seriously 'blowing it', haven't we *already* blown it?

SCORE = 90

30.
THE INDISCRIMINATE USE OF MULTIPLE 'WOO WOOS'

30. THE INDISCRIMINATE USE OF MULTIPLE 'WOO WOOS'

There's no social gathering or any other event of any description or kind (public or private) in any place on the planet that doesn't suffer from the inanity of the indiscriminate, ubiquitous and multiple 'woo woo'.

The practice has deteriorated from marker of social acceptance to automatic reflex or knee-jerk reaction. It's bellowed out in a high-pitched squeal (even by the blokes) and in a manner that makes 'Aussie, Aussie, Aussie, oi, oi, oi', and 'Aw, mate!' sound polished and sophisticated.

- *Borrow a book from the local library: woo woo!*
- *Buy a bottle of milk (the one with the dollop) from the local IGA: woo woo!*
- *Take the garbage bins out on Sunday night: woo woo!*
- *Hand out balloons at a kids' birthday party (not me): woo woo!*
- *Successfully manage to coax a golf ball (hit by someone else) to 'get in the hole' (it's a golf ball FFS - where else is it supposed to go?): woo woo!*
- *Manage to cook a dozen snags on the barbie: woo woo!*
- *Fart (without too many regrettable backside aftershocks or tsunamis): woo woo! (I can sort of forgive that one)*
- *Eat a pie while driving and without spillage: woo woo! (I can **TOTALLY** forgive that one)*

Whatever happened to a simple, sedate, and polite round of applause? A mild clap of appreciation and recognition without a recurring up-down-up-down standing ovation?

A sincerely felt, firmish handshake with either sex? Completely acceptable. A single and firmish pat on the back? Yep, that'll pass, provided the hand doesn't stray down towards the bum region and attempt to make a statement.

Woo woos reduce us to a bunch of mindless dills. It's plainly ridiculous.

Guys and girls, stop it, now!

Woo woo!

SCORE = 93 (AND CLIMBING INFINITESIMALLY WITH EACH ADDITIONAL 'WOO')

31.
FLIES (PARTICULARLY THE BLOW VARIETY)

Who decided that it'd be a great idea to place flies on this Earth? There must be someone we can blame. We're good at that.

And, why do flies have such a weird fascination for human beings? Or, is it just part of their job description? Why the hell don't they just bugger off and leave us alone? Or, buzz off in the case of the blowfly. Can someone please take them to one side, sit them down and explain to them (with appropriate and well-targeted buzzwords – sorry, terrible pun that one) that we don't find their behaviour in the least bit tolerable or acceptable?

Basically, and I'm sorry, crudely, don't we just want them to fuck off?

Supposedly, they're of some entomological importance, but all flies succeed in doing is send me into a flying fit of rage. I can spend an entire afternoon chasing a single fly around the house (with a fly swat, rolled up newspaper, tea towel, broom, pair of used undies, egg beater, vacuum cleaner, chair, couch, or anything else within easy reach) before I finally corner the irritating little shit, belt the daylights out of it and create an interesting wall mural/ink blot test in the process. (A number of the walls in our house require a serious re-paint job. But not by me.) If there's a fly in the room, I won't stop until it's wiped from the face of the Earth.

At one time during my life (which, annoyingly, seems to be dragging on forever – I need to fast-track it, now!), I lived and worked on rail construction sites in the Pilbara

31. FLIES (PARTICULARLY THE BLOW VARIETY)

region of north-west WA. The heat in the summer months was almost unbearable.

Unimaginably worse were the dreaded Pilbara flies.

There were swarms of them, literally in their hundreds, and even when I doused myself with Desert Dweller, one of the insect repellants of choice 'up North', it was never entirely effective. The wretched little buggers seemed keen to stick around, and masses of them would still buzz around my face, even if they were more reluctant to land.

The only advantage of going for a run into the hot, throat-burning desert wind every afternoon after work was that the flies were repelled for a short time, only to re-acquaint themselves on the tailwind return leg.

By the time I returned to my donga after each run, my face, neck and arms would be caked in a sticky blend of red-brown desert dirt, drenching sweat, insect repellant, flies and other insects of varying sizes and shapes that had stuck solidly to me, resembling the blotchy patches of tissue paper that dotted Norman Gunston's pallid phiz.

SCORE = 92

Ok, there's one notable and obvious exception to my intense (almost neurotic) hatred of flies. I sincerely hope one day to meet the now famous and much-loved fly that landed on Mike Pence's head, and stuck around peskily, during the 2020 US Vice-Presidential debate – like a rogue sultana irritatingly embedded in a bowl of vanilla ice cream.

I'd love to shake his 'hand' (the fly's not Mike's.) Such exquisite timing! Onya Louie!

32.
THE WEARING OF BASEBALL CAPS BACK-TO-FRONT

C'mon. Literally, you *cannot* be serious.

It never ceases to amaze me that the wearer of the reverse baseball cap seems to have no inkling of how unbelievably ridiculous he or she looks. And the older the wearer is, the more tragically comical is the look. (There's some truth in the adage, and I speak from considerable personal experience here, that 'there's no fool like an old fool'.)

Whatever possesses them to think for one microsecond that they appear anything other than just plain daft?

It's not in any way fashionable, hip or cool. That said, if it were, I'd be even more violently opposed to it, for obvious reasons. It's abject stupidity that condemns the wearer to appear like a half-baked dill. (ScoMo, please don't try it. The standing of the office of Prime Minister has already been diminished and damaged enough in recent times. Stick to brandishing lumps of coal instead, or wear *them* back-to-front on your head if you desperately feel the urge.)

If I had the balls (a ballsy person I am not – just a grumpy one), I'd confront every reverse-baseball-cap-wearing person – in the manner in which Tony failed miserably to shirt-front Vlad – and give them the rough end of my tongue, after which I'd carry out a much-needed fashion adjustment, super-gluing the offending cap to their head in the process, so that they couldn't

32. THE WEARING OF BASEBALL CAPS BACK-TO-FRONT

un-reverse the reversal of the reverse that I'd just inflicted upon them.

I'd be doing a great service to humankind, wouldn't I?

Or is it just *me*?

SCORE = 93

33.
PLANE TRAVEL (AND SMALL CHILDREN ON PLANES)

33. PLANE TRAVEL

As you know, I'm not overly fond of plane travel. In fact, it's right up there with crowds, snakes and all the other ninety-seven things outlined in this volume that roundly piss me off.

I've already made mention of my 14-hour flight on QF 0093 back in April 2017. The flight was jogging along brilliantly until it was actually time to take off. After that, it spiralled out of control downwards, so to speak.

I'd gone through the usual scoping ritual that we all undertake as we assess who of our fellow passengers, as they march single file down the aisle, would be mildly tolerable to sit next to:

'Oh, please God, not him' (I'm temporarily religious when it serves a selfish purpose).
'Oh, please God, not her' (I keep it up until I get a positive response).
'Yes, you pass, just.'
'Bugger off, stinky'.
'No way, get fucked, fuck off.'

At almost the last possible opportunity, a red-faced couple belted down the aisle and plonked their butts next to me. This was an annoyance, though unavoidable, in itself. The wife/partner sat next to me in the middle seat. Almost immediately, it became painfully obvious that she was unwell.

I was travelling overseas to run the Boston Marathon.

I didn't need to be sitting next to someone with a cold for the remaining 13 hours and 59 minutes. The first time she sniffed (and there were to be gazillions more) I winced. Audibly it seems, as she fired me a withering stare. When she sneezed, I almost leapt out of my seat. When she reached for the Codral Cold & Flu tablets, I almost wet my pants.

There's *nothing*, I repeat *nothing*, remotely pleasant, appealing, or even moderately tolerable about plane travel. Aside from spluttering co-passengers, it unfailingly includes:

- *Wailing, out-of-control children (and parents who don't give a toss, mainly because they've just rendered themselves completely, and perhaps understandably, pissed beyond repair or remorse).*
- *Dreadful food (soggy, falling-apart beetroot and feta sandwiches anyone?) which even if semi-edible, is impossible to negotiate, even for the most dexterous, which I'm not, particularly with two tucked-in arms.*
- *Cramped seating and no dotted lines down the arm rests to delineate territorial sovereignty.*
- *Blatant abuse of the cabin baggage entitlement.*
- *Dreadful (spray painted) toilets, especially post the eight-hours-of-use stage.*
- *Uncaring, unreasonable and inconsiderate bozo fellow passengers (Boofheads 1 and 2 accompany me on **EVERY** flight.)*

33. PLANE TRAVEL

- *The same drongo fellow passengers who uncaringly laugh out loud while watching a comedy show on the in-flight TV.*
- *Hoof-stomping flight attendants (mild apologies here, must be a shit of a job).*
- *Flight delays, even when your plane has been parked up overnight – did the battery go flat?*
- *TV screens that conk out 20 minutes before the end of a movie. (Can someone please let me know how* Manchester by the Sea *ended? Cheers.)*

I beg you. Just give me a parachute and let me jump. When push comes to shove, I'm happy to be pushed and shoved and take my chances.

SCORE = 96

34.
AGEISM: IT'S NOT FUNNY

34. AGEISM: IT'S NOT FUNNY

In April 2012, I celebrated my 60th birthday, not by running the Boston Marathon as hoped (I had to wait another five years for that simple pleasure), but at work in an office donga on a remote rail construction site in the Pilbara region of north-west WA.

I reckoned I'd done a sterling job of concealing its arrival (I was the oldest crew member on site by quite some distance) until I let slip the fact that I'd reached this milestone a couple of weeks after the actual date. I was quite touched that someone had gone to the trouble to arrange a cake – until one of my 'colleagues' proudly, and publicly of course, announced that the '9' on the cake had been wrongly placed upside down.

One morning, I arrived at work to find that someone had stuck up on the office wall, for all to see and laugh at, a picture of Grandpa Munster, to whom I was supposed to bear a striking resemblance. The photo had my name on it and was placed there by a guy who professed to be a friend.

On more than one occasion, I was 'lovingly' referred to as 'old timer', whereupon I'd smile and chuckle along with the joke. But inwardly I was cringing at the same time, as you do. It was marginally too close to the bone for someone continually flirting with the edge and, at other times, barely hanging on.

It was a standing joke that I was the only person on site who needed a walking frame as standard PPE. This kind of banter is a joke to most but never to the person on the receiving end. It's firsthand experience of how ageism works out there, sometimes insidiously and sometimes blatantly, in the real world.

As it happened, there'd be further, demoralising swipes at my age over the years on other construction sites on which I worked, particularly as I staggered towards 65 and beyond. On another site my nickname was Monty, 'affectionately' bestowed upon me after Montgomery Burns, the nasty, hateful and decrepit old character from *The Simpsons*.

At another time, at our customary early morning site 'pre-start' meeting, a trivia question would be asked:

> *'How many ships were in the First Fleet?' to which the comment would be added: 'Come on Ross, you should know this one, you were there!'*

(Incidentally, this 'joke' was delivered by the site HR Manager!) It's insulting, hurtful, emotionally debilitating, totally unnecessary and it *has* to stop.

And, guess what, unlike racism or sexism (as abhorrent as they are) if you indulge in ageism, you unwittingly denigrate your future self.

SCORE = 96 (AND CLIMBING WITH EACH SUCCESSIVE YEAR)

34. AGEISM: IT'S NOT FUNNY

P.S. I can almost hear what some of you out there might be thinking. 'What a hypocrite. What happened to his freedom of speech philosophy? He can dish it out, but he can't take it.'

Fair comment, to a point.

But I *did* say, in relation to the right to free speech, that I'm unsure where the boundary sits. If pushed, I'd say it lies somewhere near the 'First Fleet' joke. To place the incident into context, the joke wasn't a one-off, spur of the moment, slip of the tongue. The attack lasted for months (*'Ross, what was it like working for Tutankhamun when you were building the Pyramids?'*) It was very public, relentless, and calculated to hurt. And, over time, it did. Not that I ever dared to show it.

That's a reasonable place to draw the line.

35.
CLOGGED STRAWS (PAPER OR PLASTIC – SAME CATASTROPHIC RESULT)

35. CLOGGED STRAWS

I have the same issue with straws whether they're plastic or paper.

They clog. Except that the paper version becomes both cloggy *and* soggy.

Especially when I indulge myself with a berry or banana smoothie or the greatest drink ever invented by humankind (who cares about the calories) – the chocolate malted milkshake with a large scoop of vanilla ice cream thrown in for good measure.

I've been on planet Earth long enough (so I'm regularly reminded and warned) to work through the process reasonably successfully. To a point. Initially, I de-dunk the straw so that it only occupies the top half of the drink container. It makes the slurp idiot-proof, even for me. But, problems arise as soon as the tide starts to turn and retreat. By this time, all the truly yummy bits have settled, sunk or clumped together at the bottom of the container, and negotiating the rest of the drink is like sucking wet cement from a blocked drain with a didgeridoo.

As the saying goes: when the going gets tough, the tough get going.

That's rubbish, at least in my case. I lose it, big time. The blood rushes to my brain and any sense of logic and ordered thinking disappears in a puff of smoke. Instead of removing the uncooperative straw and then the obstruction like any rational person, weirdly I do the complete opposite, like an unthinking, petulant, muffin-deprived two-year-old on a plane. I summon every remaining scrap of energy I can muster and perform an almighty reverse-suck.

It doesn't take a superior intellect to visualise the result of this infantile behaviour.

I wear glasses.

As far as I'm aware, they don't make windscreen wipers for glasses. They should. (Another source of irritation, perhaps?)

My level of annoyance at the realisation that the reverse suck has been a mega fail pales into nothing next to the flying fit of pique I descend into in forlornly trying to clean a sloppy film of chocolate malted milkshake off my prescription specs, or the banana chunks or assorted berry bits from a thick, hand-knitted woollen jumper lovingly created by Mrs B.

SCORE = 89

36.
POLITICIANS

100 THINGS THAT PISS ME OFF

SCORE: TAKE A GUESS!

37.
SLAMMING DOORS AND SHIT-FOR-BRAINS SLAMMERS

You'll no doubt gather by now that I'm possessed by enough disturbing neuroses to easily qualify as the sole subject at a week-long psychologists' convention in Bali. Preferably, a non-volcano spewing week.

You'd be forgiven for thinking that any person who, with no perceptible effort, can think up 100 things that piss him off must, on the face of it, be batshit crazy. Of course, you'd be right, though I don't admit it to everyone – only to the three people who know me, and who knew it anyway. Most other people guess it themselves within seconds, and without the slightest encouragement.

In addition to all the others in a seemingly endless list of oddities, I'm absurdly sensitive to noise. Having said that, I still fail to understand why people obviously consider it more difficult to close a door quietly than it is to let it slam shut or, worse still, slam it shut deliberately.

Let me spell it out as simply as possible so that even the dullest dimwit may comprehend:

You – open – a – door – by – pulling – the – handle – down – (or – turning – the – knob – depending – on – the – relevant – handle – design) – and – releasing – the – door – latch – from – the – strike – plate – in – the – door – frame. After – you've – entered/departed – you – close – the – door – by – (gently) – returning – the – door – latch – to – the – strike – plate – in – much – the – same – fashion.

It really is that easy. Don't let a self-closing door self-

37. SLAMMING DOORS AND SHIT-FOR-BRAINS SLAMMERS

slam, just because it's easy/convenient/unthinkingly lazy to do so.

This is uncaring and totally unacceptable, whether you're a nut job like me or otherwise.

SCORE = 97

I strongly suspect that serial door slammers are the same people who drag chairs across floors, rather than go the 'extra mile' and actually pick the chair up and quietly place it where they want it.

There would be way too much additional effort involved, obviously.

38.
WINDOWS ROLLED DOWN IN TAXIS: THE CAT. 5 EFFECT

38. WINDOWS ROLLED DOWN IN TAXIS: THE CAT. 5 EFFECT

I find taxi drivers to be members of a unique and strange breed, and Uber drivers even more so.

Like hairdressers and nervous nellies in lifts, the everyday taxi driver insists on engaging in conversation (gratuitous or otherwise) which, as you know, is a major problem for me.

But, wait, there's more.

When you first jump in, the cab is often hermetically sealed (and, let's be honest and politically incorrect again, occasionally smelly, due to multiple, over-functioning body parts). Without warning, consultation or agreement, however, many taxi drivers seem hell-bent on changing the weather conditions inside the cab by rolling the windows down, as if they're doing you a huge favour. Whereupon, the overall ambience inside the cab is instantly converted to Category 5 Tropical Cyclone status.

If you weren't having a bad hair day before you hopped in, you'll sure as shit will have one by the time you finally escape (it's catastrophic for the swished hair over one shoulder look – see Thing 42), having waited longer for the driver's credit card device to work than the duration of the trip itself. By which time you've missed your flight. Well, at least that's a plus.

WTF?

SCORE = 89

P.S. My refusal to sit in the front seat of a taxi next to the driver should in no way be seen as a thumb-up-the-bum sense of superiority on my part. It's simply my way of hosing down the possibility that the taxi experience might escalate/degenerate into an exchange of mobile numbers or a future coffee catch-up date.

Just drive the car, dude.

39.
USING THE PRESENT TENSE TO DESCRIBE PAST EVENTS

An infuriating wank, no less.

Especially when used in history documentaries. It's the past, goddammit. It's perfectly happy to stay there! And, we should be content to let it be.

Not every event needs to be cast in the here and the now. Most of us are intelligent enough to cope with history lessons being presented as if the particular event *actually* happened way back. Like, centuries ago. We don't desperately need to feel we were there at the time our friend (and part-time narrator), Neanderthal Man, was chasing down tonight's dinner. That doesn't make it any more realistic for us. It happened in the past. We get it. We really do.

As for books written in the present tense – if I'm browsing a bookshop and happen to pick up a book that's written in the present tense, I immediately shove it back on the shelf without a second thought.

Arguably pretentious on my part? Regardless, these books are, for me, completely unreadable.

SCORE = 94

P.S. If he chose to, the **ONLY** person entitled to get away with this infuriating habit and assault on the senses is Sir David Attenborough.

40.
THE POGO DANCE (THE UP AND DOWN JIGGY THINGY)

Strange as it may seem, fishing is an activity that *doesn't* piss me off. In fact, I'm a great believer in the philosophy that there's no such thing as a bad day's fishing.

Some years ago, I trekked for hours along Seven Mile Beach in Tasmania to spend a day fishing at the junction between Georges Bay and Pitt Water. By about 4:00 pm, I was ready to pack it in. I knew I faced a long walk back along the beach in fading light, but there was enough time, or so I thought, for one last cast. All dedicated fishermen engage in the same forlorn ritual, and more than just one final cast too.

Bang! I'd hooked a sizeable flathead. That 'bang' was repeated another eleven times over the next hour or so, the end result of which was a dozen very keepable fish. They must've all been coming home from the pub, half cut, and suffering the post-pub munchies. Virtually every time I cast, they would bite. It was going off, and so was I, though not quite to the point of going viral.

I even performed, embarrassingly, a little jig up and down on the spot (I think it's called the 'pogo dance'), like sporting teams irritatingly do after they've won some major championship, even cricket teams, I'm sad to say. I reckon it looks absurd, especially when some members of the team refuse to jig at the same time, and therefore upset the team's jig-sync, or remain immovably jigless and glued to the spot.

A note to the blokes out there about the up-and-down-jiggy thingy: the Diamonds, the Opals and the

40. THE POGO DANCE

Hockeyroos (and certain African tribesmen) might get away with it (and so they should, especially those African tribesmen), but not you beefy boys. Forget it guys. Stick to the footy.

And, please, I beg of you, stop holding hands with little kids as you trundle onto the field. Remember my experience with those tiny, mischievous mitts?

Whoever thought up *that* daft practice?

SCORE = 92

41.
LOUD AND AGGRESSIVE PEOPLE

41. LOUD AND AGGRESSIVE PEOPLE

For someone who continually strives to 'go placidly amid the noise and the haste', loud and aggressive people really are 'vexatious to the spirit' and I routinely go out of my way to avoid them. I move to another seat. I cross the road. I hop off the bus well before my stop – yes, really – and walk home. I hide under the bed for the afternoon and wait for them to pass. Otherwise, I just disappear.

I'm not by any means what you might call 'chatty'. You would've no doubt guessed that by now – if, indeed, you've read this far. If so, many thanks. You're almost halfway: played strong, done good!

Apart from the massively self-indulgent diatribe that is this book, I generally only comment or express an opinion when I'm asked to – which is itself a rare occurrence. Most people are quite content with their own opinions and don't need or want mine for emotional reinforcement. And, so they shouldn't. On those rare occasions when I do speak, I've been known to talk utter rubbish.

I can happily last for hours without so much as a murmur, except internally. I've even been known to go days without talking to another soul, if I happen to be on my own for any length of time. This is pure bliss for me, a source of genuine solace, calm and a mental detox. For better or worse, the notion that 'people need people' has minimal application to me. This condition most likely has some kind of psychological diagnosis attached to it. It can't in any way be normal, can it? But, I've never bothered to have it professionally explained to me, let alone treated.

(Incidentally, I did see a psychologist for a short time many years ago. I stopped attending once I realised, alarmingly, that she was a first-class fruit loop herself and actually in desperate need of *my* help – an horrendous thought as I'm sure you'd agree.)

You may readily understand, then, that loud and aggressive people are a disturbing and debilitating assault on my senses. They smack me between the eyes and belt me around the ears without even being conscious of it, reducing me to a state of hyperventilation with a racing pulse.

Strangely, the loudness and aggression can be either hostile or jovial and *still* be confronting. It's entirely within reason, mine at least, to be loudly aggressive in the nicest possible way and still offend. Once the assault is underway, I can think of nothing else than to retreat as far away as possible. I *have* to find a quiet place to repose and, usually, a good book to live in.

Weird? Precious? A serious condition requiring psychoanalysis and expert medical treatment, including a range of prescription drugs? Just plain sooky sooky la la? Probably all of the above at various times but, nevertheless, inescapably real for me.

Loud and aggressive people: please keep your distance.

I'll gladly go out of my way, and yours, to reciprocate.

SCORE = 97 (AND SOON TO REACH THE PERFECT 100)

42.
SWISHED HAIR (LEFT OR RIGHT – SAME COMICAL RESULT)

42. SWISHED HAIR

(*Writer's note/spoiler alert: OK, I know I could cop a shit load of grief for this one. But, no, despite how this will come across to some, I'm not a sad, old white male telling women how to wear their hair. Whether that's accepted, however, is of no concern to me at all.*)

As a fashion trend, dare I say even a virtual style icon these days, the over-one-shoulder swished hair look is, for me, ridiculous.

It's right up there with the reverse baseball cap. Do females have any clue how side-splittingly laughable this looks? Especially when the hair is far too short to be swished, thereby rendering the locks un-swishable and the swisher appearing even more gormless.

You see it countless times on TV, and elsewhere. A woman can be caught in the middle of a war zone, be involved in a major life-threatening drama or otherwise be enduring some type of diabolical, nightmarish catastrophe and, yet, the hair will, nevertheless, be swished to one side (more times to the left I've noticed, with adjacent right ear exposed to reveal the must-have earring) for the sake of appearance (and/or the camera, and/or the upcoming selfie). And, even when the swisher is otherwise resplendent in steel capped boots and a hard hat!

Even if style trends *are* so important to them (and we all know that, bizarrely, they most assuredly are), can't women think up something, anything, with more visual appeal than this one? If you have loads of luxurious locks, display them to the world in all their glory, I say. Don't hide them away in a single strand of (sometimes) gnarly-looking twine draped over one shoulder or the other depending on which way the wind's blowing.

I can think of only one spectacle more visually ludicrous and that's when, admittedly rare, this dopy ritual is perpetrated by a male. Yes, I've actually seen it!

SCORE = 93 (OR 100 IF THE OFFENDER IS A MALE)

P.S. It's also asymmetrical, which for a nut job like me is particularly irksome.

Further, sad, old white male explanatory note: I'm making a point about image, fashion trends and superficiality. If females feel the overwhelming need to wear their hair draped to one side, no problems, freedom to choose, go for it.

43.
STINKY PERFUMES AND AFTERSHAVES

Whatever possesses people of either sex to blindly and arrogantly assume that they can invade another person's personal space with their own overpowering brand of noxious pong?

'I stink, therefore, I am'? (Apologies to Descartes)

Why must their presence still be felt, and smelt, two hours after they've vacated the building or, worse still, a confined space such as a lift, or an already smelly taxi?

For the sake of those of us who have a hypersensitive olfactory system and find your personal habits way less than tolerable, can I please ask you to find less intrusive ways to 'make a statement'. Mind you, must you really insist on making a statement in the first place? More on that precious nugget later.

If what you bathe in, or liberally splash yourself with before you leave the house, is a 'reflection of your personality', sadly I venture to say, it just may be that your personality needs to undergo a significant overhaul, if not a total reconstruction.

Please stop it, now!

SCORE = 95

P.S. You won't believe it, but I actually prefer the smelly taxi cab.

44.
THE MALFUNCTIONING PHOTOCOPIER

If the truth be known, and it's out there somewhere, photocopiers get more pissed off with me than I do with them.

They see me coming. And they despise me. They cringe, cower and skulk in the corner of the room hoping they won't be spotted. But, there's no escaping. I can, with the aid of that hypersensitive olfactory system I mentioned, sniff out the fear felt by a photocopier a mile away.

(Coincidentally, I once drove across the Nullarbor in a campervan, accompanied by a dog, our pie-loving Welsh springer spaniel, Taffy, and a photocopier. Don't ask me to explain the circumstances – they're way too freaky. Suffice to say, photocopiers are cold and aloof objects with the personality of a cement truck. When I pause and think about it, I can't *really* see why we have nothing in common. Anyway, I can vouch for the fact that they're hopeless to cuddle up to at night.)

I've already mentioned that I have no rapport with anything vaguely mechanical. I must exude some kind of weird, cosmic, anti-magnetic force (much as I seem to do with people) that causes any kind of gizmo (and any kind of person) to pack it in if I get within spitting distance, more often than not in the form of a seismic paper jam (in compartments A, B, C, D and E).

I've spent more time on my back unblocking photocopiers than I have changing car tyres. So much so that, on one not so memorable occasion, it was assumed by

44. THE MALFUNCTIONING PHOTOCOPIER

several office staff that I *was* the photocopier repairman.

In the end, however, I do what most other chicken-shit people do in the same situation. Once I've convinced myself that the photocopier is completely stuffed (about 7 seconds after I've gently tapped the 'copy' button), I wait 'til no one's looking then run like the dickens back to my desk and pretend I have no idea what the hell happened *this* time to the uncooperative beast. Or, for that matter, the identity of the person who cocked it up in the first place. (*'Search me. It was like that when I tried to use it.'*)

SCORE = 89

P.S. My innate ability to render machines totally unusable is in no way confined to photocopiers, or can openers if I knew how to work them. I possess extensive skills over a wide range of other mechanical objects. My mechanical cock-up resumé includes, but is in no way limited to: dishwashers, ovens, vacuum cleaners, electric jugs, TVs (in which I specialise and have an honorary trade certification), computers (a unique expertise there, too), espresso coffee machines (of course), and anything with two or more wheels. (Hang on, you'd better throw unicycles in there as well.)

I was *not* a repairman in a previous life (if the job involves anything more than a role of sticky tape, forget it) and will *never* be employed by Retravision, the Good

Guys or Harvey Norman in their electrical departments, or otherwise.

But, I *am* kind to animals.

And, photocopier repairmen.

45.
THE 'NO WORRIES, NO DRAMAS, TOO EASY' REASSURANCE

Don't be fooled. Instead, be painfully aware that the subject matter of this gem of simplistic re-assurance *will always be* a huge worry, *will always be* a drama of Melbourne Theatre Company dimensions and *will always be* so inherently complicated and difficult to achieve that it'll take a unanimous UN resolution just to arrive at first base.

Apart from being an insincere throwaway line for the unachievable or the exorbitantly expensive, the use of the expression has a darker purpose. It's basically used, intentionally, to get rid of you!

The true meaning of 'no worries, no dramas, too easy' is, essentially, as follows:

> *Listen mate, I seriously don't want to do this job because it's not worth my while and, in any case, I really have no clue how to get it done. I'm only telling you otherwise to get you off my back so that I can go and quote another job that's vaguely doable with my limited and laughingly dodgy skills and will actually bring me in some reasonable dollars in the shortest possible time with the least possible effort. I won't answer your calls, so don't bother chasing me. Bugger off!*

'No worries' = Be very afraid.

'No dramas' = Be terrified out of your mind.

45. THE 'NO WORRIES, NO DRAMAS, TOO EASY' REASSURANCE

'Too easy' = You're much better placed staying in bed for the day, and handing over your user ID and password.

SCORE = 91

46.
AUTOMATICALLY BEGINNING SENTENCES WITH 'SO'

46. AUTOMATICALLY BEGINNING SENTENCES WITH 'SO'

Soooooo, where do I start with this one?

Indiscriminately beginning every sentence with 'so' is not only irritating, it makes no grammatical sense.

It's one of those annoying habits that people fall into unconsciously. It dumbs down discourse between otherwise reasonably intelligent individuals and seems to be used, or misused, when a person isn't confident about the point they're trying to make or when he or she needs to buy time to think up a half-plausible response to a straightforward question.

It's a totally unnecessary addition to what should be an intelligible, believable and well thought out sentence or statement.

Sadly, however, I'm pushing shit uphill with this one, as I would be if I protested loudly (or at all) about that other excruciatingly dreadful habit of adolescent girls* commencing every sentence with 'like'.

Or, having 'like' as the *whole* of the sentence!

Or, bleating out 'thank *yo*' when, of course, they *really* mean 'thank *you*'.

Jusayin'.

SCORE = 93

*Ok, soooooo, I admit that this awful habit isn't confined to adolescent girls. Nevertheless, *they've* somehow, like, managed, like, to turn it into, like, an art form.

47.
THE STACKS-ON-THE-MILL FOOTY FALL DOWN

47. THE STACKS-ON-THE-MILL FOOTY FALL DOWN

You'll identify with this one, I'm sure.

Seconds after a player scores a goal and performs the obligatory, and highly choreographed, knee-slide towards the throng of rapturous sideline supporters (in itself, an immense irritation), he/she is enveloped by the rest of the team which, collectively, feels the urge to play stacks-on-the-mill on top of the not-at-all-camera-shy goal scorer.

Do we really need to see this? Does it have to happen at all? Bizarrely, the scoring of the goal has now become an irrelevant sideshow preview to the knee-slide/stacks-on-the-mill main attraction. Should the goal scorer continue with football or is he/she (and, for that matter, the rest of the troupe) better suited to a career with *Cirque du Soleil*?

Isn't just watching the footy good enough? Or, can't we cut to a commercial (maybe one promoting physiotherapy or knee replacement surgery?) while the knee-slide/stacks-on-the-mill is being performed live?

Eventually, someone will get seriously injured performing this for-show, look-at-me nonsense. Don't look to the likes of me for sympathy when it occurs. And what really happens on the bottom of the scrum that we don't, thankfully, get to see? What's going on down in there? Just boys being boys/girls being girls, a bit of hanky panky maybe?

Yeah, nuh. Don't wanna know.

SCORE = 93

48.
OPINIONS (INCLUDING/ ESPECIALLY MINE)

48. OPINIONS (INCLUDING/ESPECIALLY MINE)

'We enjoy the comfort of opinion without the discomfort of thought'
– John Fitzgerald Kennedy
(Commencement Address, Yale University,
11 June 1962)

Opinions? They're vastly overrated ... in my opinion. Including, or perhaps especially, mine. You would've gathered that by now.

In reality, as the JFK quote suggests, most so-called opinions are little more than ill-considered, venting-session rants. As the saying goes, opinions are like arseholes. Every person has one. And, many people quite obviously have arsehole opinions.

Being a loud and vocal drongo should never be mistaken for being a person who has a carefully considered, well thought through and intelligent opinion.

I'm not sure what happened to the 'mind-your-own-business-and-keep-your-opinions-to-yourself' approach to life, but, in any case and sadly, it's long gone. Now, life is a relentless quest to give, and be forced to receive, largely irrelevant or unwanted feedback. Bellow like a bull (even semi-articulately) just because you can, but in reality, say nothing. Talkback radio has a lot to answer for.

- *'Have your say'* (you don't have to be asked twice)
- *'We welcome your comments'* (not me)
- *'We'd love to know what you think'* (huge assumption here)

- 'Post your review' (and destroy a perfectly respectable business just because you can)
- 'Join the conversation' (oh God, please don't)
- 'Tell us how we can improve' (which we'll ignore because you're wrong and, in any case, it's not politically correct to tell the truth and hurt our feelings)
- 'Stay on the line to complete our quick, two-minute survey' (in reality, a lie of Trump-like proportions)

Still, consistent with my free speech philosophy, go ahead and say what you like. Knock yourself out. Just don't expect me, or anybody else for that matter, to take any notice, much less be convinced, or persuaded by, or even comprehend what you say.

Say what you like, but accept and expect that there will be consequences.

SCORE = 92

49.
POWER PRAMMING YUMMY MUMMIES

(Yeah, okay, I'm setting myself up to be slammed on this one, too.)

Whatever.

Back in the day, in a galaxy far, far away, you pulled the folded pram (actually no more than a 'pusher') from the boot of the car, gave it a bit of a shake and, in true transformer-fashion, the cute, lightweight little gem magically presented itself, fully assembled, in front of you on the footpath.

You then plonked young Sally or Billy somewhere in the middle of the contraption and continued on your merry way. The whole exercise took about 43 seconds.

Not now.

That'd never do for young Zot, Skylah, Rocket or Racer, or for their thirty-something mum, the spectacularly clever Rebekkkkkkahh. Or, she assumes quite matter-of-factly that she's spectacularly clever merely because she's recently given birth.

I've no idea why this particular generation of females gives the strong impression (to me at least) that they're the first and only generation of females to have ever produced offspring. Is it a misplaced sense of self-importance – or am I just being a totally unreasonable, cranky old fart? No doubt Rebekkkkkkahh and her BFF's will find my comments rude, wide of the mark and grossly offensive. And, I hope, politically incorrect.

Nevertheless …

49. POWER PRAMMING YUMMY MUMMIES

- *Why do they feel the urge to take up every square centimetre of a footpath or the entire aisle-width of a supermarket?*
- *Why do they feel compelled (with little or no apparent consideration for others) to steamroll their way along cycle paths in two-abreast convoys?*
- *Why do they need such monstrously huge prams in the first place? (Sorry, 'little people transporters'.) Is it a symbol of status and entitlement (the baby pram equivalent of the four-wheel drive), or am I, again, being way too harsh, way too petty and way behind the times?*

Yes?

Too bad. Don't care. Bekkkkkk, this one's for you.

Ode to Rebekkkkkkahh

Dear Bekkkkkk, you are so clever
As you embark on your endeavour
To show the world
That you are quite the mum

Despite designer pram and baby
Don't you think that maybe
Your rock star life is really
Just ... 'ho hum'?

Decked out in tights and boots
With a swagger no one disputes
You prance and preen
As if you rule the world

Well, I've got news for you, dear Bekkkkkk
As you continue on life's trek
It won't continue as it started
Or unfurled

It'll be a huge surprise
On the day you realise
That giving birth is common
Nothing more

When the penny drops, dear Bekkkkkk
An epiphany by heck
It'll dawn on you:
'It's happened all before!'

SCORE = 93 (OR 63, IF SOMEONE CAN PROVE TO ME I'VE GOT IT ALL WRONG, OR 43 IF YOU BELIEVE THAT TAKING ON THIS FORMIDABLE DEMOGRAPHIC IS JUST WAY TOO LIFE-THREATENING).

50.
THE UNDERSUPPLY OF MILK IN HOTEL ROOMS

Upon entry into a hotel room, most normal people check the quality and comfort factor of the bed. Then, whether the room comes with a reasonable number of cable TV channels.

Not me.

I head straight for the mini-fridge and scrutinise the mini-milk supply.

I like my coffee with plenty of milk dumped in. Even if I didn't, the typical hotel supply of those dinky little thimble-size containers of milk is still woefully inadequate.

I don't even stop to unpack – the suitcase, I mean. Instead, I unload. I call reception, room service, housekeeping, the concierge, his grandma, security, the poolside cabana guy, *his* grandma, the events manager and anybody else listed in the hotel directory (probably the same person, not including granny) and order every container of milk in the hotel's possession. I then scour the floor on which my room is located for the kind, caring but non-English-speaking room attendant who, *because* of the language barrier, is only too pleased to give up his/her entire trolley supply of milk just to get rid of me. I've even been known to enquire whether the hotel has a resident cow on the premises and, if so, how long it'll take to send it up.

Gimme milk, and lots of it. Otherwise, I go ape-shit and troppo all at once. And, that's by no means an attractive visual spectacle.

50. THE UNDERSUPPLY OF MILK IN HOTEL ROOMS

By the way, my pissed-off state gets launched into the stratosphere if the only milk on offer is the skim variety. Drinking skim milk is like having a shower in a raincoat. Any person who offers you skim milk out of preference is a person who can never be trusted. Like men who wear cravats. Or bow ties. Or leather hats (with or without bobbly corks). Or braces. Or flip-up sunglasses. Or bum bags. Or long socks and sandals. Or singlets of *any* description.

Or a hideous amalgamation of two or more of the above, displayed tragically and disgracefully at or about the same time.

SCORE = 93

Half way!

You made it!

Woo woo!

51.
WORDS LIKE 'GOURMET', 'LUXURY', 'EXOTIC', 'FIVE STAR', 'PARADISE' AND 'EXCLUSIVE'

For me, the sound of words like these (there *are* others, like all the bullshit buzzwords we've talked about) is no less excruciating than the sound of a fingernail being scraped and screeched across a classroom blackboard.

Overly neurotic, you say? OK, you've got me there. Nevertheless, let me ask you this:

How many times have you indulged in a 'gourmet food experience', pampered yourself at an 'exotic luxury day spa' or enthusiastically taken up a 'once-in-a-lifetime exclusive offer' only to be left with an overwhelming sense that you've been:

- *Irreversibly disappointed?* (like being served a slice of underdone toast)
- *Undeniably ripped off?* (like buying a Royal Easter Show bag)
- *Unquestionably underwhelmed* (like at 00:01 am on New Year's Day) or
- *Embarrassingly sucked in?* (like wearing tight-fitting undies).

Or worse still, a demoralising combination of two or more of the above, like being served a piece of underdone toast, while stripped down into tight-fitting undies at the conclusion of an underwhelming New Year's countdown.

Seriously, is the experience ever as gobsmackingly wonderful as the picture paints it?

For instance, is so-called 'fine dining' *ever* what it's

51. WORDS LIKE 'GOURMET', 'LUXURY', 'EXOTIC', 'FIVE STAR', 'PARADISE' AND 'EXCLUSIVE'

cracked up to be, or is it just an anti-climax of biblical and shamefully over-valued proportions, leaving you pissed off, still hungry, and in search of the nearest McDonalds?

Never felt this way?

Never, ever?

I think you're telling porkies.

SCORE = 91

52.
HAVING TO CONVERSE BEFORE 11:00 AM

52. HAVING TO CONVERSE BEFORE 11:00 AM

There's something unspeakably jarring about a smiley-faced cheery chops who insists on engaging in conversation before 11:00 am.

Suffice to say, I'm not a morning person (mind you, I find it a grind having to negotiate other parts of the day too) and can't for one second abide any person who is. Even the sound of the word 'morning!' delivered with a tone that is vaguely optimistic, pleasant or upbeat, is enough to sink my already ordinary disposition into the depths of abject depression from which there is no chance of recovery. Even with the aid of copious quantities of mega-over-strength coffee.

I'm not, as you would've gathered by now, a perpetually perky person. 'Today is the first day of the rest of my life'? Really? You *cannot* be serious! Please, I just need you to fuck off!

For the sake of my fellow human beings for whom I have the greatest respect (?), I really should chuck on a sandwich board each morning bearing words to the following effect:

> *Highly dangerous, particularly before 11:00 am (WST). Approach with extreme caution. If sighted, be aware that this foul and grotesque creature has escaped from the Perth Zoo. In case of an emergency, tranquilise with caffeine (or a chocolate malted milkshake if caffeine is unavailable).*
>
> *Call 000 immediately. Run. Fast.*

Just keep your distance folks. Don't give even the slightest indication that you'll utter a word, or even a syllable, in my direction before 11.00 am (WST). Give me space to walk on the left-hand side of the footpath and on the left-hand side of the road, without obstruction, and we'll both be over-the-moon with joy.

Well, as joyful as I can be at that time of the day, which is in no way joyful at all.

SCORE = 94

53.
HAVING TO CONVERSE AT ALL

I never hang around afterwards, anywhere, for a chat, assuming I've been dragged there, wherever it is, in the first place. I don't long for a mag. I don't yearn for a yarn, ripping or not so ripping.

Mind you, do people actually *converse* these days, or do they merely engage in banter and one-liner one-upmanship? In any case, although it's completely academic in my case, I'm crap at banter, too. The clever retorts elude me. I often think of something snappy to say two days after the event. By then, it's a bit problematic to hit the 'replay' button.

I've never been 'one of the boys'. Whenever I pluck up enough courage to speak in such groups, my words stumble, fumble and dribble out like incoherent, unconvincing gibberish. I've always found it difficult to get my 'message' across in a face-to-face setting or to sound vaguely believable. I can see the disappointment in their glazed-over eyes. They tune out. They switch off. I register zero on their credibility-ometer.

Whatever.

I've never learnt, or bothered to learn, the 'art' of small talk. I am, however, a great exponent of the ask-questions-and-listen principle when necessary, mainly because it's an easy way to avoid saying much myself. Just steer people onto their favourite topic (usually themselves, their team, and/or their kids/grandkids – and, even more so, their spouse) and switch off. It works most times and it's a win/win. Good for me, good for them.

53. HAVING TO CONVERSE AT ALL

And, it prevents me from having to cut short a one-way conversation and rudely bolt for the nearest exit.

A social cop-out? Plainly disrespectful? Maybe, but for me a vital shifting spanner in the personal survival toolbox.

SCORE = 95

54.
WHAT THE HELL IS A 'RELATIONSHIP COACH'?

54. WHAT THE HELL IS A 'RELATIONSHIP COACH'?

Sadly, I confess that I've never quite understood the male–female relationship despite having been entrenched/ensconced/enmeshed in one myself for well over four decades. (Mind you, all other human relationships and interactions pose considerable challenges for me too, as you well know.)

It's one of an increasing number of life issues that I've not quite come to grips with. You'd think I'd have life sussed by now, wouldn't you? Not so. I'm as confused now as I ever was. 'Wise beyond his years' and my name should *never* be mentioned in the same sentence.

The nature of the male–female relationship puzzles me constantly. My dilemma isn't made easier by the way society, or at least popular culture (whatever the hell that is), consistently deals with it. It's either treated frivolously in a sitcom, overblown in a Netflix drama series, or trivialised by reconstructing it into a cringeworthy Reality TV show. By that measure, it's difficult to progress beyond being forced to meekly accept, or spookily morph into, one or more of the stereotypes that are shoved under our noses on an endless basis.

It's been the subject of countless books, magazine articles, plays, songs, movies, TV shows and, now, all forms of social media. It's in our faces almost every waking moment of the day in some form or another. It surely has to be the single most done-to-death issue in the history of the human race. Maybe, scarily, it *is* the history of the human race. Yet, I defy anyone (male or female) to stand up, place hand on heart and declare that they understand how the male-female relationship actually works. Certainly not me.

Nor, I strongly suspect, does a so-called relationship coach, who, surely, can and should do no more than act as a 'sounding board' for a couple who really must sort things out between themselves.

I'm probably being a trifle harsh (who, me?), but I sometimes wonder whether males and females are truly, fundamentally compatible. Like, on a 'til-death-do-us-part' basis. I've even witnessed a no-holds-barred 'domestic', between two male/female competitors, a couple of kilometres from the finish of a marathon.

Speaking from my side of the fence (rather than perching limply and fearfully on it, as most men are prone to do these days), it may be that the male of the species just doesn't have the right wiring to fully comprehend the nature of the relationship, or his role or place in it, let alone deal with it as he should. Maybe males need a total re-wiring/re-education overhaul at a strategically located gulag in the middle of the Australian desert. I know just the place.

It's probably me, but I have some sympathy for the 'Men are from Mars, Women are from Venus' hypothesis, even if the theory may not be as fashionable or as widely accepted these days.

Anyway, I'd best leave it at that. I'm probably in a crap

54. WHAT THE HELL IS A 'RELATIONSHIP COACH'?

load of trouble as it is. Best let the relationship coaches out there work their magic.

Or, most likely, not.

SCORE = 96

P.S. Or is it just *me*?

55.
STAGGERINGLY THOUGHTLESS DRIVERS

55. STAGGERINGLY THOUGHTLESS DRIVERS

They really should be lined up and pelted with rotten tomatoes, and then hauled off to that gulag I mentioned a moment ago. Or, worse still, be forced to sit through a re-run of an unedited ScoMo Budget Night speech – before he accidentally got punted upstairs and, of course, in no way connived his way to the top job.

You *know* who I mean:

- *On the freeway, they insist on parking themselves out in the right-hand lane, cruising along and boxing you in at 'irritation speed'.*
- *Obviously, as their God-given right, they change lanes JUST because they've indicated and even when it's plainly dangerous to do so.*
- *They squeeze into your lane JUST because you've left a safe distance between your car and the car ahead.*
- *You stop at an intersection and give way to a car approaching on your right only to find that the goose driving it decides, without indicating, to turn left into your street.*
- *Most likely the same goose who, at the local supermarket carpark, decides to straddle two car spaces or at least uncaringly encroach onto yours with his gas-guzzling four-wheel drive tank.*
- *The bozo brother of goose number one who overtakes you on the highway at a gazillion miles per hour, then cuts into your lane, slows down and parks himself less than a car length in front of you,*

and proceeds to cruise along again at unthinking irritation speed.
- The wife/sister-in-law of goose number one and bozo brother, respectively, who, for some unfathomable reason, appears incapable of comprehending that she's kept her indicator on for the last 100 kilometres. (The indicator sign on the dashboard must've been obscured by the swished hair.)
- The eldest daughter (I think her name's Rebekkkk-kkahh) of goose number one and his dill of a wife (uncaring drivers commonly run in the family) who **KNOWS** you're waiting patiently for her car space yet **INTENTIONALLY** takes:
  - five minutes to open the boot
  - ten minutes to place her 37 half-filled plastic bags of groceries into the boot
  - ten minutes to strap young Zot into the designer baby car seat
  - five minutes to grope around in her handbag/shipping container to find the car keys
  - three minutes to re-swish the hair
  - two minutes to re-adjust the rear vision mirror (which needed no adjustment in the first place)
  - two minutes to put her seat belt on
  - three minutes to get all nice and comfy and re-position her bum

55. STAGGERINGLY THOUGHTLESS DRIVERS

- *two minutes to engage the 'R' (she's half-forgiven there)*
- *three minutes to ACTUALLY reverse*
- *thirty seconds to stop and wave goodbye as she's leaving*

By which time, of course, the shops have shut.

The list goes on and on. As we know, there's no limit to the idiot buffoons driving cars out there who, obviously, have no clue how to drive courteously, or how to drive at all. Or how to successfully eat a pie with both hands on the wheel.

Drive safely and, if you possibly can, do so without boiling rage!

SCORE = 92

56.
THE BULLSHIT JOB INTERVIEW QUESTION: 'WHAT ARE YOUR SALARY EXPECTATIONS?'

56. THE BULLSHIT JOB INTERVIEW QUESTION

Sorry to all you personnel recruiters and HR people out there in employment land (no, I'm not really), but this one's just a giant cop-out, and I never directly answer it whenever I'm unfairly put on the spot.

Without wanting to sound ageist (in any case, I'm allowed to at my age), I'm afraid I'm old school when it comes to recruitment. If you're an employer and you advertise a position, **YOU** are the one who sets the terms and conditions of employment. **ALL** the terms and conditions, not just **SOME**. Don't leave it in the hands of the job applicant to awkwardly fill in the gaps. He or she may have no real insight into what salary you may be offering, or even what the market rate for the position might be.

And state the salary or salary range, when you advertise the position. Don't leave it to the interview stage. If you're fair dinkum about recruiting, present a *complete* offer, including the salary on offer, not just a half-arsed one. If you don't, the applicant should have the right to decline to answer, or to tell you to shove the job up your backside.

If I *had* to answer, I'd give anything to spruik something along the following lines:

Listen, sport, my bank desperately needs me to squeeze every spare cent I can out of you. If you MUST know what my salary expectations are, have a chat to one of my dear friends at the bank (now that they've finished giving evidence at the Royal Commission and provided they're not already behind bars) and work out between you what it's going to take to cover the mortgage(s) and leave a few bucks over for once-a-week chicken and chips.

And, for heaven's sake, *make* a decision! Quickly. How hard should the recruitment process be? You advertise. You shortlist. You interview. You make a decision. What's with this multi-level procedure involving a 'screening interview', a first round of interviews, a coffee catch-up, followed by a second round/bullshit 'behavioural assessment' (which I never pass for obvious reasons) and, then weeks of further delay before a decision is made? Often, by then, there's been a complete internal company restructure and the position you applied for, was interviewed for, and recommended for, no longer exists.

It's really not that hard, guys! Go with your gut and your common sense. If the he or she who you eventually recruit turns out to be a complete dud, you can always punt them at the end of the probation period.

Make it happen!

SCORE = 93

P.S. How's this for a (real life) HR gobbledygook, double-speak job application rejection:

'Our feedback is that we felt that you interviewed well for the position and would have skills and experience that would add value to this function. However, in this case we are exploring another potential option for the position,

56. THE BULLSHIT JOB INTERVIEW QUESTION

and will move forward with this candidate at this stage. This is not a reflection on your experience, we just feel that this profile is a closer match for the current business requirements.'

A simple: 'Sorry, mate, it's a big no' would've been quite sufficient. I'm a big boy. I can take it. Most times.

By the way, I won't let on where that real-life recruitment-person quote came from. Suffice to say, the employer in question was a very Big Australian.

57.
SPASMODIC AUSTRALIAN-NESS

57. SPASMODIC AUSTRALIAN-NESS

I've never felt the overpowering urge to prove, or display, my 'Australian-ness', whatever that may actually mean.

With all due respect to those who do, I don't feel the need to drape myself in the Australian flag (or stamp an inky, temporary Aussie emblem on my forehead or cheek), on any particular day of the year, to evidence the fact that Australia is the country where, accidentally and fortuitously, I was born, and where I've lived my entire life.

Though some blatantly work hard at it, I am not, nor could I ever be, a 'professional Australian'. I much prefer, for instance, to reflect and pay my respects on Anzac Day quietly and personally. It's no less meaningful, to me at least.

I've never 'celebrated' Australia Day as such, partly because of the inherent ambiguities and contradictions it throws up. I certainly don't see it as nothing more than an excuse for a giant piss-up. Or, as a once-a-year opportunity to drag the Aussie cricket shirt or the boxing kangaroo rugby jumper out of the cupboard and proclaim to be a 'proud Aussie'.

I'm not able to adequately articulate what it means to be an Australian – how could I if I have no point of comparison? – or, more accurately, what it *should* mean. Tolerance. Kindness. Respect. Good humour. Social inclusion. An absence of pretension. Broad equality. Meaningful reconciliation at all levels. An acceptance of all races, religions, sexual orientations and age groups. A sense of fundamental fairness. An open and honest recognition of our history. A (healthy) irreverence toward authority figures. It's all of these qualities and more, which, to be clear, are characteristics of many countries and nationalities. They're not exclusively or uniquely Australian, I strongly suspect.

But, what I *do* know is that Australian-ness isn't what you do, say or how you behave on any particular day of the year, and certainly not what you deliberately and cynically practise at rallies or in front of TV cameras to further your own narrow self-interests.

If it can be labelled at all, it's who you are (who you *really* are and not what you conveniently *think* you are) and how you behave – subtly, silently, unconsciously and without the need for recognition – *every* day of the year. It's a set of fundamentally fair and decent values and principles that guide how life is lived continually and consistently at a practical level.

Not just when it suits a highly dubious, self-serving or plainly reprehensible cause.

SCORE = 95

58.
'UNSUBSCRIBE' BUTTONS THAT DON'T

I rarely subscribe to anything. I'm not a big-time consumer. I'm not a 'joiner' (for Groucho Marx-type reasons). I don't get, hopefully, sucked in easily. Mind you, apathy may play a huge part here, too. But, like most of us, I find a constant need to 'unsubscribe' from offers for a product or service that I haven't subscribed to in the first place.

Having to go through that exercise is quite sufficient to piss me off, especially when, to do so, you're often required to navigate your way through a labyrinth of portals and dead ends before you get there.

It's the last straw, though, when, having hit the unsubscribe button, you're asked to log in to complete the process. I didn't subscribe in the first place, so how *could* I have a username and password? Equally infuriating is being told, dismissively: 'Can't find the server'. How many different ways can I tell you to get stuffed? Not my problem. Just 'unsubscribe' me!

And, finally, *'You've been successfully unsubscribed,'* is one of the greatest lies ever perpetrated on humankind. Never believe it. It's crap on a mega scale. Fake news. As sure as eggs, sometime in the next few weeks or months, the offer for the same ghastly product or service will sneakily rear its ugly head again and result in you having to endure the torture of the unsubscribe process all over again.

SCORE = 89

59.
BADLY BEHAVED SHOPPING TROLLEYS

I get them every time.

Even when I've test driven and changed models three or four times before I summon enough courage to venture into Coles or Woolies (and do battle with Bekkkkkk), I'm still landed with the impossible-to-steer model whose wheels are so out of kilter that, if I'm shooting for aisle seven, I inevitably end up in aisle thirteen or the next door bottle shop.

They have minds of their own, don't they? No matter how carefully you shepherd them along, they always travel in whatever direction they please, especially when you attempt the impossible and dare to round the corner into the next aisle. They're designed, fabricated and placed on this earth to intentionally piss you off. Me in particular, it seems. It's their sole mission in life. And without doubt, they do.

And what is it about the excruciating clickety-clack noise that each confounded contraption makes? No matter where you are in the supermarket, you automatically attract the kind of attention you don't want. In my case, that's any attention at all. Without fail, people stare at you with that patronising expression that says:

> *'You pathetic loser. You got the one that makes the annoying clickety-clack noise. Why didn't you change models like the rest of us? Like any sane or sensible person? What kind of idiot are you?'*

59. BADLY BEHAVED SHOPPING TROLLEYS

Just a common garden-variety idiot, apparently.

SCORE = 89

60.
FERAL KIDS IN SHOPPING TROLLEYS

60. FERAL KIDS IN SHOPPING TROLLEYS

While on the subject of uncooperative shopping trolleys, this entry is a contribution from my equally crazy cousin, Ian. He and I grew up together on the northern beaches of Sydney. We have a lot in common, apart from being related.

Like me, Ian is on the wrong side of 60, and he considers it his right, having gone through the rite of passage of middle age, to be grumpy and roundly and routinely pissed off. It's what he's worked hard all his life to achieve. He's earned his stripes through countless years of tough slog. Now, he's arrived and he has a few things to offload, such as the following that really pisses him off:

*Kids with smelly arses and toxic shoes (or no shoes at all) who sit in shopping trolleys at the behest of their moronic parents; this is the place where I need to put my **FRESH** food!*

He's bang on, of course.
Go cuz!

SCORE = 88

P.S. The smelly arse element of the above is commonly an unwanted by-product of the two-day old disposable nappy that's mysteriously found its way down to the ankle region of Grotty Kid Number 1, and left its mark, literally, on the bottom of the shopping trolley.

61.
PEOPLE WHO STAND IN DOORWAYS OR TWO ABREAST ON ESCALATORS

61. PEOPLE WHO STAND IN DOORWAYS

Not a biggie for me, this one, but more than just a mild annoyance, nevertheless.

It's a great example of people who simply have no peripheral vision, zero concept of the presence of others, or who otherwise just don't give a shit.

When confronted by this experience my tactics are direct, obvious and, in my view, entirely appropriate to the circumstance. I proceed on my way and strategically creep up behind such folk and position myself within a micro-millimetre of the back of their heads. Admittedly, this grosses me out somewhat but it's only temporary, before I bellow, fractionally below noise-pollution level but still with an unnaturally cheery twang and a forced smiley face (both of which are exceptionally difficult for me to perform and, and in any case, go against my 'better nature'):

'EXCUSE ME PLEASE!'

This has two desired and wholly positive consequences:
1. The offenders automatically part like when Moses did his Red Sea thing; and
2. It scares the living crap out of them.

A unilateral win/win.

And, I have to confess, moderately entertaining enough to set me up for the day, provided it's after 11.00 am.

SCORE = 83

62.
SIRI: WHY WON'T SHE GO OUT WITH ME?

I'm the sort of person who can set out on a harmless, leisurely stroll around the neighbourhood only to return several hours later, after becoming hopelessly lost and only just stopping short of dialing 000 (if I'd ever thought or bothered to have a mobile with me), with assorted cuts, bruises and abrasions to various parts of the body. Or, sporting the results of some other minor disaster or general act of uncoordinated clumsiness.

Warning: Never, ever put me in charge of navigation, not even if it involves negotiating a short, straight line to somewhere familiar. For me, getting from point A to point B usually involves a pre-journey pep talk, a two-hour DIY workshop with a road map and heaps of Googling.

GPS? Forget it.

Siri is incapable of understanding nuance. Never plug in a single destination name. Plug in 'Venus Bay', and you could end up in South Australia, not on the Gippsland coast of southern Victoria. Plug in 'Interlaken', and you have a better than average chance of ending up skiing and honing your yodelling skills in central Europe, four months later, not touring central Tassie as intended. Plug in 'Texas', and guess what?

Consequently, Siri and I aren't the best of chums, though I do find her voice moderately sexy in a robotic kind of way. I've asked her out for a coffee catch-up date once or twice but, sadly and coolly (like an unplugged photocopier), she only ever tells me to take the first exit at the next roundabout.

62. SIRI: WHY WON'T SHE GO OUT WITH ME?

SCORE = 84

By the way, Siri, you're quite often an irritating, nosy little twerp. So, butt out and mind your own friggin business. If I want you, I'll call for you. Ok?

63.
BAD GRAMMAR, MISSPELLING, AND EMAIL MADNESS

63. BAD GRAMMAR, MISSPELLING, AND EMAIL MADNESS

I can't abide bad grammar. It sets my teeth on edge, inflicts a diabolical, incurable, red-raw skin rash and makes my hair fall out (well, more than it does already).

There's simply no excuse for bad grammar. None. Not even in this I-don't-give-a-stuff-what-I-say-or-how-I-communicate-as-long-as-I-get-my-message-across kind of world.

I especially can't cope with spelling mistakes and miscellaneous typos that appear in the 'news tickers' at the bottoms of TV screens. Surely it doesn't take much to get *them* right? A quick spell check before they're posted?

For some weird reason, bad grammar annoys me infinitely more when someone from the ABC blurts it out. Notwithstanding program and staffing cutbacks, a subject that could well have its own entry in this book, *they* should know better, shouldn't they?

And, if you feel inclined to ever send me a text message (allow at least seven days for a reply), please refrain from using 'r', 'u', '2', '4', 'thx', 'atm', 'plz', 'tbh' and other similarly ridiculous and lazy abbreviations.

The home of bad grammar and poor communication (aside from Facebook and Twitter) is the humble but highly misused, not to mention downright dangerous, email. Why do people find it impossible to express themselves clearly, concisely and unambiguously in an email? I can't fathom the reason for it.

Emails are not the place for the quick blurt. They're not the place for people to write as they think. Heaven forbid. Yet, many people do just that. Take your time. Relax. Think it through before you go off half-cocked, and end up confusing or offending all 257 receivers of your communication and then have to spend the next two days retracting and back-tracking, regardless of how many 'lols', 'smiley faces' or other emojis you may have to use to explain yourself, or embarrassingly seeking forgiveness.

If you feel you don't have the time, or in fact don't have the right level of skill to get your message across without, unintentionally, causing WWIII, pick up the phone.

Or, better still, go and have a face-to-face with young Xander and Marigold (hairdressing is just their weekend job) who are, after all, located at the next couple of pop-up work cubicles adjoining yours anyway.

Btw, please exercise due skill, care and discretion before you hit the *'Reply All'* button. Most people are only peripherally interested, or, let's be honest, really don't care or want to know.

SCORE = 94

64.
FLAT-PACKED FURNITURE

If I have to buy an item of furniture and find that it requires any kind of assembly, I simply don't buy it at all.

I point to the already made-up version on the showroom floor. If the salesperson is reluctant to sell it to me (mainly because *he* has no idea how to assemble the replacement item), I leave the shop immediately. There's good reason for it. I'm totally incompetent (in an all-thumbs kind of way) when it comes to putting something together, so I won't put myself and the people around me (all one of them in the form of Mrs B) through the agony.

Even if I possessed a moderate amount of manual skill, which I don't, I'm even more hopeless at deciphering instructions, especially when they've been translated into fake English from classical Swedish.

Can someone please get back to me on the following:

- *Why you're not advised that you'll need to take long service leave, and possess an advanced degree in engineering, to assemble the wretched item?*
- *Why you're not advised that you'll need to spend an entire afternoon in Bunnings buying all the tools needed for assembly, and still have to return at least four times for things you've missed?*
- *Why, amongst the 628 individual items that come spewing out of the box (one of which takes aim and breaks your left little toe), there's a mega oversupply of part A17, but no parts B43, C12 or D71?*
- *Why, when you've finally overcome all obstacles that are deliberately placed in your path, the queen*

64. FLAT-PACKED FURNITURE

size bed you thought you'd purchased has, in fact, not so magically transformed into a TV stand with matching coffee table?

Get stuffed IKEA.

Don't ask *me* for a testimonial.

SCORE = 92

65.
THE ABUSE OF SOCIAL MEDIA

65. THE ABUSE OF SOCIAL MEDIA

Trust me, I *do* get why so many people become so attached to, and even obsessed by, social media.

I readily acknowledge its benefits and the positives. It's a real joy for many people and a powerful tool to promote social discourse and change. It has launched careers and given entrepreneurs a voice and a channel to promote their talents and creativity. It's a constant source of social inclusion for millions. It acts as a conduit and a connection. It's even been instrumental in toppling repressive political regimes.

Thoughtfully and selectively used, it's massively important to those who feel the need to share progressive ideas, culture, art, family news, music and current events and to build virtual communities.

I get that, even though the benefits of social media don't, by my choice, directly affect or interest me. Thankfully, I'll never face the dilemma of being unable to filter my 'social feeds'.

But, as we're all too aware, there's an unfortunate flipside, an ugly dimension to social media. Is the social convenience worth the bullying, vitriol and abuse that pours out through the many and various social media outlets on a regular basis? I'm talking about:

- *Slut shaming*
- *Trolls*
- *Trump (before the ban)*
- *(Genuine) fake news*
- *Racism*

- *Inciting violence*
- *Mindless gossip*
- *Malice*
- *Trump (before the ban)*
- *Intrusion*
- *Sexual harassment*
- *Personal intimidation*
- *Body shaming*
- *Banality*
- *A senseless and shallow platform to vent*
- *Trump (before the ban)*

Does social media do more harm than good?

I'm not in a position to answer that question with any authority. I'll leave that one hanging in the breeze for you to join the dots. Better still, I'll leave it to be answered by the expert social commentators and pop culture critics out there. They're sure to have an opinion. Whether or not it's an informed one is another matter.

Suffice to say, it's something I'll never take up, let alone 'embrace'.

SCORE = 94 (BUT ONLY IN RESPECT OF ITS ABUSE. OTHERWISE, FOR THOSE WHO TREAT IT WITH RESPECT AND USE IT AS IT SHOULD BE USED, ENJOY)

66.
UNCARING LIFTS

Without doubt, lifts are the most menacing and infuriating mechanical devices known to humankind – apart from photocopiers and the new fancy can openers.

Like a wonky-wheeled shopping trolley, each lift has a mind of its own. And a decidedly malevolent 'ghost in the machine' one at that.

Please explain:

- *Why the lift I've been patiently waiting for descends 17 floors at warp speed, stops at the floor immediately above mine and then determines not to move for the next three hours? (or, alternatively, buggers off in the opposite direction!)*
- *Why, when I've pressed the up or down button on my floor, the useless pile of shit sails straight past without so much as a 'Chill. I'll be back in a minute'?*
- *Why, when the lift does arrive at my destination, the doors take an interminable amount of time to open, or simply don't? (And, the same useless pile of poo then, without notice, takes off again)*
- *Why, after I've entered and pressed the button for my destination, the doors open and close 47 times?*

Associated grizzles:

- *Someone who yells out to you to 'hold the lift' (generally without a 'please') and then proceeds to saunter to the door carrying on a loud conversation on their mobile phone.*

66. UNCARING LIFTS

- *Someone who 'instructs' you to press the floor button for them.*
- *Someone who, upon entering the lift, asks you whether it's going 'up' or 'down'.*
- *Someone who **MUST** squeeze themselves into the lift when there's clearly no available space and then inanely blurts out 'got room for a skinny person?' which they're plainly not, probably never were and most certainly never will be.*

No wonder I'm much happier to take the stairs. Except after I've trudged up 13 flights only to find that the entrance door to the floor is locked.

Some days, it just doesn't pay to get out of bed.

SCORE = 91

67.
PEOPLE WHO TALK TO YOU IN UNCARING LIFTS

67. PEOPLE WHO TALK TO YOU IN UNCARING LIFTS

To expand upon the previous topic, why do people insist on engaging in conversation in lifts? It's nothing more than a nervous reflex, I suspect.

I've made it a cast iron rule of grumpiness to never talk to people in lifts. You'll understand, then, why I've been known to vacate a lift several floors before my destination on the faintest suspicion that 'good morning' might develop into a full-blown conversation.

Perish the thought. Especially before 11:00 am.

People, bless them, can't help themselves in lifts, can they? The compulsion to engage is irrepressible. It must have something to do with the confined space. They *have* to speak. Plainly, they have an overwhelming (though, in my case, misplaced) sense that it's discourteous *not* to acknowledge their fellow passenger. Averting your gaze, an art that I've perfected over many years, makes squat difference.

You can tell a 'blurter' as soon as they enter the lift. He/she must, simply must, find something, anything, to say. It gets too much for them as they fidget for the right words. Their face turns bright crimson. Sweat drips from their brow. Veins in their neck threaten to rupture. The watch gets adjusted. The mobile gets an extra compulsive fondle. The tie gets straightened. The hair gets re-swished. For them, silence isn't golden. It's excruciating. After about 45 seconds, the pent-up pressure and emotion becomes intolerable. They blurt. And, they invariably blurt absolute nonsense, clearly demonstrating the depth and breadth of their anxiety.

Hot Tip: If you spot me in a lift, relax, chill out and enjoy the ride in the comfort that I certainly won't be offended if you keep it to yourself, whatever it is that you're bursting to share.

SCORE = 92

68.
AUTHORITY – EXCEPT FOR THE LOLLYPOP MAN

I'm inherently ambivalent about many things but particularly so when it comes to authority figures.

I've never had a pit-of-the-stomach feeling of respect for people in positions of authority, especially when the exponents of it take themselves seriously, as many do. The more earnest they appear (and this attitude generally reflects their perceived importance of their position in the world), the more comical they tend to look. Particularly when they jibber-jabber complete, but nevertheless carefully rehearsed, rubbish at a press conference, flanked by a bunch of smugly grinning, noddy-headed hangers-on who often nod when they should shake, and vice versa.

Generally, though, I've resigned myself to go along with authority figures, but not with any great enthusiasm or conviction, I have to say. Something like a cross between Ned Kelly and the Black Knight from *Monty Python and the Holy Grail*.

However, I *do* draw the line at the lollypop man or lady at the school crossing, and the road works 'spotter'. He or she commands my full respect and attention and I'd gladly strip naked or hold my breath for two hours (or both) if they demanded. As authority figures, I readily concede that they serve an immensely worthwhile purpose. So, you'd better throw the cops, dentists and travel agents in there as well, I guess.

On the other hand, I have a simplistic and decidedly naïve inclination to thumb my nose at most other authority figures, whoever and whatever they represent. My almost overwhelming urge is to scream out: '*Bugger off! Why should I listen to you, let alone heed what you say?*' (or something far less polite).

I'm not a good follower. I don't readily fall into line. My inclination is to do the complete opposite. The only reason I tow the line and therefore remain moderately employable is the (massive-incentive-to-behave-myself) money factor. I'd be a rubbish devotee or member of a mass movement, social, religious or otherwise (a crowd problem there as well). And I could never be convinced to accept the teachings of a so-called guru. I'd rather stay at home and find enlightenment by reading a good book or going for a long run, or going for a ride on a train (one of my favourite things to do).

With an authority problem the size of Uluru, it beats me how I ever became a lawyer.

I might try to explain it in Volume Two.

SCORE = 95 (AFTER THE WANKER COMPONENT IS FACTORED IN)

69.
BANKS

69. BANKS

SCORE = INSERT YOUR OWN (BUT IT SHOULD BE BLINDINGLY OBVIOUS)

70.
BROAD BEANS AND RELATED BOWEL IRRITANTS

70. BROAD BEANS AND RELATED BOWEL IRRITANTS

In reality, they crap me off more than piss me off.

Apart from all her many other remarkable skills, Mrs B is a keen and successful grower of all kinds of veg. Aside from the usual suspects such as carrots, tomatoes, broccoli, peas, cauliflowers and potatoes, a favourite of Mrs B is the humble broad bean. They grow anywhere, everywhere and prolifically in our veggie patch. Consequently, they're indiscriminately added to every dish that happens to find its way onto the meal table, including soups, stews, salads and, when I'm not looking, they're blended and mixed into drinks, muesli and all manner of dips and spreads.

Now, for someone who already has a robust constitution and is as regular as clockwork (we're talking twice a day here, folks), overdosing on broad beans, particularly when mixed with gravel-like muesli interspersed with other broad bean meals, doesn't sit well at all with me. Actually, 'sit' isn't quite the right word. The nuggety little buggers don't sit at all, they travel straight through at a very rapid rate like a juiced-up, out-of-control Ferrari.

I'm the one who does the sitting, so regularly the clock can't keep up. I positively percolate with a proliferation of prodigious, potent pulses.

Crap to that!

If I'm not running, sleeping, or working in the garden, you know where to find me.

SCORE = 87

70A.
BRUSSELS SPROUTS (OR ANY KIND OF LENTIL): SEE THING 70

71.
RUBBISH ADVERTISING: NOT HAPPY, JAN!

I'm of two minds on this one. (I really must stop this continual ambivalence. It's starting to piss me off.)

Let's not mince words, though. Advertising, essentially, is the means by which organisations try to convince you (whether through, say, a retail outlet, online, TV commercial, or teleshopping ad), to buy, subscribe to, watch, participate in, sign up for, or otherwise 'consume' a product or service that's often of little practical use, benefit or interest to you or anyone else. And where it is of some use, it breaks two hours after you finally extract it from the impenetrable box or wrapping in which it's packed (see Thing 72). Or, it turns out to be a total disappointment (see Thing 51).

Even if advertising is creative (by way of jingles, slogans or catch-phrases), it uses the same basic, strategic, persuasive, message-pumping techniques as any other form of propaganda. It's behavioural manipulation employing a highly emotive message that zeroes in on the base human instinct to accumulate or consume, or find a measure of comfort in doing so.

Essentially, advertising is the business of flogging stuff that, let's face it, commonly and sadly ends up in landfill.

As the well-known quip goes, more often than not, if you do purchase something, you end up with stuff that you don't really need in an effort to impress people you don't really like and invariably pay for it with money you don't really have.

71. RUBBISH ADVERTISING: NOT HAPPY, JAN!

Most forms of advertising are atrocious and insulting to even the most basic level of intelligence. Its jarring, in-your-face, con-job ugliness is a truly disturbing feature of modern living.

However, there are exceptions. There are, very occasionally, absolute gems:
- The *Rhonda and Ketut* AAMI ad
- The *Not Happy Jan!* Yellow Pages ad
- The *Great Wall of China/Emperor Nasi Goreng* ad
- The *One with the Dollop* milk ad (my all-time favourite for what it's worth)
- The *Bugger* Toyota ad

These are clever, standout exceptions to the rule.

Trouble is, they tend to be lost in a sea of embarrassing, turgid and puerile rubbish.

SCORE = 91

72.
MODERN DAY PACKAGING

72. MODERN DAY PACKAGING

Back in the day, items that you purchased, cheerfully and without your right arm being twisted halfway up your back, were thrown into a brown paper or string bag or wrapped in newspaper or shoved into a simple-opening cardboard box (assembled by our two-year-old 'friend') with a single strand of sticky tape to keep the box shut.

After you arrived home, it took all of 3.5 seconds of effort to retrieve your purchase. Then, you were 'good to go'. At the very worst, a pair of rusty scissors or a blunt bread knife helped to complete the task.

Not anymore.

Nowadays, even the humblest item is vacuum-sealed, shrink-wrapped or seemingly cryogenically embalmed and densely packed to such an infuriating extent that removing it from its impenetrable encasement involves proficiency in the use of a razor-sharp scalpel, a chainsaw or a nuclear-powered jackhammer. Or, a combination of all three, after two of them break. And, the agonising unwrapping process commonly takes up the whole of the Easter long weekend. Or, you're required to obtain access to the item strictly by virtue of a code that's sent to you via SMS about three weeks after you've purchased it and hulked it home with the aid of a $200-a-day Thrifty rent-a-truck.

It even takes me about two and a half hours, and the entire contents of the top two cutlery drawers, to remove the vacuum-sealed cap from an instant coffee jar. I can understand why packaging is made 'child-proof', or even 'idiot-proof' for people like me, but why does it have to be made 'everybody-proof'?

I know life wasn't meant to be easy. But, does it really need to be *that* hard?

Or is it just *me* (again)?

SCORE = 88

73.
OVER-THE-TOP CONSUMERISM

A consequence of my aversion to the persistent blather of bad advertising is that I'm not a natural or dedicated consumer. Or, for that matter, a casual consumer. I don't strive to acquire. I don't feel compelled to fill my life or surroundings with the latest gadget, mechanical device or other miscellaneous 'stuff'.

I don't need or want the newest anything (except when it comes to running shoes). And, let's face it, that newest thing isn't built to last in any case. Generally, it's built to last only as long as it takes for us to forget that we purchased the item very recently. And, just long enough for us to decide that we *must* purchase another replacement item (but the upgraded, and more expensive, version) because a 'celebrity' of dubious substance and importance has somehow convinced us that we simply can't do without it.

In short, I'm an advertiser's nightmare. And, I admit, I contribute only minimally to Australia's GDP which, of course, is how we measure our prosperity and, hence, our 'happiness quotient' these days.

On the contrary, I'm almost perpetually in declutter, de-junk mode. One of life's pleasures for me (admittedly, there aren't many) is to discard and strip down, whether on a physical or emotional level. To 'get rid of', or simply acknowledge that I don't 'need', is a great and wonderfully cleansing joy. Frugality is a virtue, not a hardship. It's sensible, responsible living, not weirdo fringe-think.

73. OVER-THE-TOP CONSUMERISM

Do we really need all that we acquire like out-of-control, drunken bowerbirds?

Surely, as praiseworthy as it is, we wouldn't need to be so self-conscious about recycling if we didn't consume so much in the first place? And, why are we regularly scolded in the media for not keeping our side of the GDP bargain? *'The economy is suffering because people simply aren't buying.'* Good, I say!

One day, I'll go completely 'off the grid' and put a ruthless, full-blown anti-consumption theory into practice.

I mean it.

I *really* do. But, that's another story. And, for another day.

SCORE = 94

By the way, I'm not a huge consumer of food either. My personal observation is that we eat much more food than we need to. To me, maybe simplistically, it's a calories in/energy out proposition. Is there any more to it than that?

We *can* do without and survive with less, can't we? This would mean we would waste less and emit less carbon (about $10 billion worth of food is dumped in landfill annually, apparently).

(Except for chocolate malted milkshakes.)

74.
THE LOGIES: WHO ARE THESE PEOPLE?

74. THE LOGIES: WHO ARE THESE PEOPLE?

Very little needs to be said on this one, don't you agree?

What words could possibly do justice to describe this abysmally woeful wankfest? Let's have a crack:

- *Tragic*
- *Embarrassing*
- *Boorish*
- *Cringe-worthy*
- *Crass*
- *Amateurish*
- *Banal*
- *Odious*
- *Garish*
- *Insulting*
- *Laughable*
- *Superficial*
- *Vomit-inducing*

When your gong acceptance speech, from a Logies night several years back as I recall, comprises a glowing tribute to your wife's backside, you know it's time to give reality, humility, perspective, and good taste a serious re-visit.

And please explain to me why we see fit to annually invite an overseas guest presenter who obviously doesn't want to be there, and in any case, is way too pissed to know where they are or, for that matter, what planet they're on.

Logies night is like an agonisingly (un)real life version of *The Office* (the British version) but without the subtlety, the talent, the clever humour or the genius dialogue.

No further commentary needed.

Goodnight Australia. You've been a wonderful audience.

SCORE = 93

75.
GROSSLY DISTURBING PERSONAL HABITS

Every office or workplace in the country has their fair share of irritating creatures who have personal habits and idiosyncrasies that range from the slightly eccentric to the downright gross and revolting.

Some common examples:

- *The Habitual Throat Clearer: One of life's most irritating creatures who has absolutely no idea that he annoys the living crap out of anybody who happens to be vaguely within ear shot.*

- *The Seismic Snotty Sneezer: Either of the 'repeato rapido' variety who shoots out a minimum of six sneezes at a time with machine gun ferocity or, even more disturbingly, who lets rip with a single bone jarring version that measures about 6.7 on the Richter Scale.*

- *The Compulsive Chuckler: Up there with the Habitual Throat Clearer as the world's most annoying person, they finish every sentence, or even intersperse every sentence, with a nervous giggle, especially when the subject matter of the conversation is particularly serious.*

- *The Serial Media Device User: You name it, they've got it. This person has it all and it's all on their desk at the one time – iPads, iPhones, tablets,*

75. GROSSLY DISTURBING PERSONAL HABITS

play stations, electronic organisers, two-way radios – anything and everything that's remotely electronic and makes regular beeping sounds that slice through your brain like a laser beam.

- *The Cyclonic Super Sniffer:* Someone I invariably have the misfortune to sit next to on a plane trip (with Boofheads 1 and 2 front and back) and from whom there is no escape, unless I'm prepared to perform a skydive minus parachute. ('I'll supply the tissues. Just blow your nose, dick for brains!')

- *The Chronically Convulsive Cougher:* From little wimpy ones (reasonably inoffensive) to the 'basso profundo' type, these coughs are generally emitted by smokers who sound as if they're just about to disgorge what's left of their one remaining lung.

- *The Conspicuously Cavernous Yawner:* Who feels duty bound to let the rest of the world know that they hadn't had enough sleep the night before – and usually well above noise-pollution level.

- *The Professional Nose Picker:* This person has the unfortunate and grossly disturbing habit of picking his nose, and if he doesn't scoff them on the spot or deposit them under his desk for afternoon tea, he rolls them into disgusting little balls and flicks them into the never-never ... and invariably landing onto your desk.

- *The Warbling Whistler:* This one performs their own signature 'trill' at the end of each recital. It's impossible to make out the actual tune that's being whistled but you know for a cast iron fact that you'll have the same nondescript tune rattling around in your head for the next several days, and subconsciously perform it, and curse yourself for being sucked in so easily.

Any of these strange and infuriating creatures currently lurking about in your office or workplace?

Let me know.

I'll arrange to have them visited in the early hours.

SCORE = 96

P.S. There are, of course, many others: pen clickers, foot tappers, casual strollers, knuckle crackers, chip chompers, soup slurpers, keyboard thumpers, movie chatterers, tooth pickers, walking texters, perpetual perkies, brazen belchers, noisy nose blowers, phantom farters, nail clippers, flab flaunters, nostril snorters. Naturally, I *could* go on.

Maybe Volume Two?

Or, Volumes Two and Three?

76.
THE 'TALL POPPY' ACCUSATION: WHY WE GET IT WRONG

In my view, this is a hugely misused concept on which we commonly miss the mark.

Irreverence is, thankfully, an integral part of the Australian 'fabric'. We don't easily stand on convention. We happily take the Mickey and gladly take the piss. We occasionally have a dig at even the loftiest, mightiest and most gifted among us. Hopefully, and for the most part, it is both given and taken in good humour.

But, if we see someone with talent and high standing in a particular field who, despite their accomplishments, gets 'too big for their boots', I seriously believe that most of us don't consciously seek to tear them down. We don't set out to intentionally punish or destroy. We just remind such folk, in no uncertain terms, to pull their head in, to not get ahead of themselves and to stop acting like a truculent child – in other words, like a goose.

Once their feet are back on the ground, it's business as usual and we'll readily and regularly forgive and forget, no more, no less.

But, do it again sport, and we'll jump all over you once more and remind you who you are, where you came from and who you should be thankful to.

So, look out.

SCORE = 89

77.
COMICALLY (UN)FASCINATING FASCINATORS

Right up there with the reverse baseball cap, the fascinator has to be the most ridiculous and inaptly named fashion item ever conceived. It's not a quirky bit of fun. It's garish, gross and grotesque all at the same time.

As a temporary diversion: when was the last time you spent any length of time in a caravan park? If 'never' is your answer, bear with me anyway. There's a point here. Somewhere.

I've already mentioned that I have no sense of fashion whatsoever, nor do I crave one. I've also made it crystal clear that I'm never going to make it onto the runway at a Paris fashion show. OK, not even Milan or New York in an off year. But, if there is one aspect of caravan park life that intrigues me the most, it's that they (and even more so free camping sites) seem to afford everyone, including me and not-so-haute-coutured Mrs B, an absolute licence to 'dress down' whenever the need is felt.

I suspect that, secretly, we all have this urge. There's a slob in each of us just dying to 'make a statement'.

If I'd ever had a camcorder (and known how to use it or hadn't broken it in the attempt), I'd love to have recorded some of the horrendous outfits that are paraded at all hours to and from every caravan park amenities block that I've ever visited.

Lilac shower caps, purple bath robes, orange trackie bottoms stylishly matched with iridescent green tops, fluffy red bath slippers, pink 'crocs', carrot-yellow and tan PJs, floral toiletry bags, multi-coloured bath towels.

77. COMICALLY (UN)FASCINATING FASCINATORS

And, as for the women...!

Then again, I reckon there are far worse looks at Flemington on Melbourne Cup day. Especially late in the afternoon after it's been bucketing down for a couple of hours and most racegoers are well and truly past the mildly pissed stage, the fascinator will have invariably managed to get strapped to its owner's ankle or become hopelessly tangled in a bedraggled mess of drenched, swished hair. Not to mention all the other bits and pieces and body clumps and bumps that've sadly and conspicuously collapsed and drifted down south as well.

And as for the women ...!

SCORE = 93

78.
THE BOWELS OF MRS B'S HANDBAG

78. THE BOWELS OF MRS B'S HANDBAG

My dear Mrs. B, W ... T ... F ...?

Do you have *any* idea what you keep in there, how long it's been there or how rancid it's become since you first placed it there three months ago?

Mrs. B's handbag is, effectively, a cross between the Tardis and the Narnia wardrobe.

On more occasions than I care to remember (because I try to shut out the nightmare), I've been requested/directed/instructed by the good Mrs B to fetch an object from the bowels of her handbag. I approach the request with an immeasurable degree of reluctance. When I *do* relent (an inevitability), I tackle the ordeal with immense trepidation – that is, with pissing-my-pants fear and dread. On the basis of many previous nightmarish experiences, I don't go in there unarmed, though. I power up with a heavy-duty facemask, asbestos gloves and a pair of high-tensile radioactive-proof metal tongs.

The trek into the black hole/vortex/parallel universe that is Mrs. B's handbag is like a journey to the centre of the earth, minus the starry-eyed wonderment. It's a Freddy Krueger version of Forrest Gump's box of chocolates. You *do* know what you're going to get and it's bloody terrifying:

- *Miscellaneous (heavily oxidised) one and two cent coins*
- *Wads of used tissues*
- *Random items of makeup of questionable age and quality*

- Two half-eaten muesli bars
- A 2-millimetre layer of assorted crumbs, fluff and feral bits and pieces of unknown origin and identity
- Three-year-old breath mints
- A set of keys that belong to our 2008 Airbnb Christmas rental
- Ticket stubs to the 1996 season of Phantom of the Opera (kept for sentimental reasons)
- More wads of used tissues (the ones used to mop the tears at the opening ceremony of the Sydney Olympics – also kept for sentimental reasons)

I avoid going in there at all costs, unless I've had a recent Ebola shot.

Or, I've hired a hit man at $1,000/hour to do the dirty work for me.

SCORE = 95

79.
BEING MADE TO FEEL LIKE YOU DON'T MATTER

I've been on the receiving end of some incredibly ordinary personal treatment in recent times, but of course I'm not alone here.

As you're now well aware, I'm a strong believer in the 'shit happens' principle. What's not to believe? Being a shit-happens denier is the equivalent of denying the existence of climate change, or flatulence, or Albania.

However, being able to shrug it off as merely a natural part of the ebb and flow of life can only be taken so far. There's a tipping point for us all. A breaking point. A stop-the-world-I-want-to-get-off point. A point past which we can't and won't be pushed, notwithstanding that human beings are, I'm convinced, an incredibly resilient bunch.

Reaching that tipping point is a contemporary illness suffered by many.

That point, that line in the sand, varies from one person to another and from one circumstance to another. It's unique and personal to each of us.

The tipping point can be a major trauma or something quite innocuous by comparison. In any case, and for whatever reason, the trigger gets pulled and we unhinge. We can't cope and we melt down, sometimes with catastrophic consequences.

Whilst I've reached the edge of my own tipping point several times in the more recent past, like most, I've somehow managed to pull myself back just in time.

Reaching the edge is often the end result of an

79. BEING MADE TO FEEL LIKE YOU DON'T MATTER

accumulation of isolated incidents of ill treatment and abuse, the combined effect of which is to be left with the feeling that you don't matter. It's a hollow and empty realisation that you simply have no worth. You feel alienated. Powerless.

The abuse, which need not be physical and may have an even greater impact if it's emotional, can come from many sources and take diverse shapes and forms. It can be cold, callous, ruthless and recurring ill treatment from a large and impersonal organisation (see Thing 69). It can be profound and continual disrespect from people who should know better. It can be the grinding humiliation of unemployment, severe financial strain, high-level stress or physical exhaustion. It can be ageism in all its many and insidious forms, or being treated dismissively, or simply not how you deserve to be treated by someone who owes you more. Or, being made to feel that you have no control, no say, and no input into decisions that affect you deeply. Or, sadly, simply being a person with a 'different' racial, sexual, ethnic or cultural disposition.

Any one of these may be enough to force you to the edge. If a combination of several of them come together at or about the same time, in an imperfect storm of suffering and distress, it's little wonder that people are pushed to life-threatening extremes.

Very few things in life have permanency. Nothing lasts forever. All things must pass. Thankfully, even nightmares are temporary. You push through the dark days and time has a wonderful way of healing. You hang in and you hang on.

But, there *are* times when you just don't think you can.

And you find yourself slipping away.

SCORE = 100

80.
LOSING AN ASHES TEST CRICKET SERIES

Many people will think I'm extremely weird (many already do!). But, sorry, this is a biggie for me.

With a few exceptions (such as long-distance running, athletics, and maybe swimming), I'm not a great follower of sport, I have to confess. There's no point asking me who 'my team' is. I don't follow either Rugby League (a game that very few other countries play), AFL (a game that no other country plays) or, for very good and obvious reasons, Rugby Union. Given my 16 years as a soccer player (even two years as a professional), it's even stranger that I don't follow the 'beautiful game' either.

- *Tennis?*
- *Golf?*
- *Skiing?*
- *Hockey?*
- *Gymnastics?*
- *Sailing?*
- *Darts?*
- *Ballroom dancing?*
- *Frisbee throwing?*
- *Baton twirling?*
- *Cake decorating?*

Yeah, nuh.

- *Horse racing?*
- *Motorsports?*
- *Synchronised swimming (and synchronised grinning)?*

80. LOSING AN ASHES TEST CRICKET SERIES

- *Lawn bowls (except the barefoot variety involving copious quantities of full-strength alcohol)?*
- *Wrestling (unless it involves mud, copious quantities of full-strength alcohol and a scantily clad Mrs. B)?*
- *Being a Weekend Viking?*
- *Muggle Quidditch?*

You cannot be serious.

But cricket? Absolutely. I loved it as a kid and have loved it ever since. Not the now-all-too-predictable, formulaic, glove-touching, crappy, limited-overs version. And, certainly, not the I've-got-two-hours-to-kill-before-I-get-bored-so-let's-watch-the-smash-and-bash-Big-Bash-game-on-TV version either.

No, there's only one form of cricket for me and that's Test cricket. And, a Test series between Australia and England is as good as it gets.

I could easily watch *every* ball bowled in *every* test. (Actually, I have.) No worries. No dramas. Too easy.

Having said all that, you can readily understand why *losing* a Test series to the Poms pisses me off beyond simple despair. It devastates me in over-the-top, totally out-of-proportion dimensions. Smoke billows from my ears. Laser death rays shoot from my eyes. My brain slowly stews, then fries. I seethe with uncontrollable bad temper, especially when the Poms perform the Pogo Dance/Up and Down Jiggy Thingy – and a very ordinary version of it, too.

I lose all sense of logic, rationality, time and space. I become unglued – not too difficult a state of being for me, though. I babble, drool and foam at the mouth. I brood, boil and bubble for days, weeks on end. I'm inconsolable. I mourn. I grieve unashamedly. I sook, whinge and sulk at truly infantile levels.

But, guess what? I'm nowhere near as pathetic as I used to be!

SCORE = 97 (IT'S BEEN AS HIGH AS 153)

81.
PUSHERINNERS

Like I said earlier, I'm old school. OK, true confessions: I'm just plain old.

I know it's bizarre behaviour, totally out of step with modern, contemporary living, and borderline new age wimpish, but I actually wait my turn. Even though I manage, with unerring regularity and whatever the circumstance, to find myself in the wrong queue.

Like the scoping ritual I put myself through just after taking my seat in a plane, upon entering a shop of any description, I immediately size up the competition and place myself roughly where I believe I am in the 'are you being served?' pecking order.

Generally, I err on the side of caution and tend to give in to others well in excess of what's reasonable or justifiable. (I have an honorary doctorate in self-deprecation from WUS University – bestowed *in absentia* as the concept of honorary degrees is something about which I have huge reservations. Crowd problem, too.)

Most times, fair-minded people go with my flow and respectfully allow me to take my turn as and when it arises. But, as we know all too well, there's a dickhead or two, in every group. This particular person goes through no such scoping exercise. Why should he? Queues and civilised order aren't for the likes of him.

When the inevitable push-in happens, my response is swift, direct and decisive. If the shop assistant looks at me with the 'I think you might've been next' expression, I announce clearly and audibly: *'No problem, serve this gentleman next. He's obviously far more important than me and rightly deserves to be treated as someone special.'*

Most times the offender squirms, shrinks and shrivels with a feeling of embarrassment and shame, particularly after realising they've pushed in past a silver-haired senior citizen.

Occasionally, however, they ark up, whereupon my courteous tone does a '180' and I let fly with a tirade of bile, abuse and hostility that even frightens the tripe out of me.

Though not wonderful for the blood pressure, again, it's not without its mild entertainment, not to mention cleansing, value.

SCORE = 90

82.
PEOPLE WHO INVOLVE YOU IN THEIR MOBILE PHONE CONVERSATION

82. PEOPLE WHO INVOLVE YOU IN THEIR MOBILE PHONE CONVERSATION

As strange as it may seem to you plainly disrespectful people, I can say without fear of contradiction that I really have no great desire to hear or in any other way be involved in any part of your conversation or be an involuntary recipient of the sad details of your tragically dreary life.

Why on earth do you believe that imposing *your* world on the rest of the world is acceptable behaviour? Sorry, I forgot, you're simply not aware that your behaviour is beyond obnoxious. Must be tough being an inconsiderate moron.

Things I really care to not know about you or your life include, but are by no means limited to, the following:

- *That your boyfriend's a first-class dick*
- *That your boss is an even bigger dick*
- *That the people you work with are a bunch of dicks*
- *The ins and outs (mostly outs) of having a mole removed from your left butt cheek*
- *What you're having for dinner (after you've told us all the intimate and gory details of the mole removal)*
- *What your plans are for the weekend, while you recover from your butt mole episode*
- *That you can't stand the latest skanky bunch of Bachelorettes*
- *That you're seriously contemplating swishing your hair over your **LEFT** shoulder from now on*

- The deep and meaningful relationship you have with your pet galah *(the choice of pet is so appropriate)*
- The shallow relationship you have with your parents *(and your first-class dick of a boyfriend).*

A mobile conversation you'll **NEVER** hear:

'Oh hi … Can I call you later? I'm on the bus at the moment and it wouldn't be fair to disturb my fellow passengers with the boring, banal and totally insignificant details of my pathetic life. Call you back in five … Kiss, kiss. Love you!'

SCORE = 96

83.
CELEBRITYISM: WHO ARE THESE PEOPLE?

I've already mentioned that my opinions are vastly overrated. They're particularly underwhelming to me.

Nevertheless, here goes (again).

We routinely celebrate the *wrong* people. And not only do we idolise and adulate the *wrong* people and the *wrong* institutions, we idolise them for the *wrong* reasons.

Why should so-called celebrities of any kind – film stars, pop singers, TV stars, royalty, footballers, and strangest of all, politicians! – command so much of our attention, let alone adulation? What inherent talents and superiority do they possess that make us feel the desperate need to not merely applaud their skills and achievements, but to place them on a pedestal as well? So she's a commoner one day and, by sheer accident, a 'celebrity royal' the next. Big deal. Why should we care? Sadly, many of us do.

Cast your memory back to the last time you heard an interview with a sad individual who'd just snatched a glimpse of their favourite celebrity A-lister. They're never able to give a rational or plausible explanation for their undying love and affection. Instead, they sob some version of: '*Oh, I don't know really. I just think she's wonderful!*'

Holy crap! Are you kidding me? What absolute tripe! Do yourself a favour and grow up, especially if you're pushing 70!

Influencers? F … F … S …!

Is it a reflection of, or reaction to, our own sense

83. CELEBRITYISM: WHO ARE THESE PEOPLE?

of personal inadequacy? Do we see in celebrities what we'd like to see in ourselves but never will? And for that matter, why do we idolise *anything* or *anyone* at all?

Sincere admiration for genuine talent and high achievement is one thing, and generally it's healthy and appropriate – the Nobel Prize, UN humanitarian awards, the science 'Oscars' are some examples. The recipients of these indeed deserve recognition and congratulations.

But fawning, fall-down bowing and scraping reverence? Really? Ask yourself: is it deserved at any level? For anyone? C'mon, we're better than that, aren't we? We have the capacity to discern and to place things, events and people, in proper perspective and balance, don't we?

As mentioned previously, I'd be a terrible member of a cult. I'd most likely hide up the back of the room and giggle to myself, or blow raspberries, or worse.

And please don't throw your hands in the air and snipe that I'm just a bitter and twisted exponent of the Tall Poppy Syndrome. That's missing my point, with all due respect (see Thing 76).

People of genuine and meaningful talent, at all levels, are interest*ed*, but do not care to be superficially interest*ing*.

SCORE = 94 (AND CLIMBING IN TANDEM WITH A GROWING SENSE OF IRREVERENCE)

P.S. Or, again, is it just *me*?

84.
TRADIES WHO DON'T FRONT UP: 'IT WAS MY BIRTHDAY'

84. TRADIES WHO DON'T FRONT UP

This has to be the lamest excuse known to humankind for not turning up to an appointment (or not showing up for work for that matter). It's also a big one for my cousin Ian. Especially when you're not warned about the 'no show' and you've stayed at home *all* day in anticipation of the pre-arranged appointment.

It's just a birthday!

I know this'll come as shocking news, but being your birthday is of no interest or relevance to me whatsoever. I have no interest in my *own* birthday, let alone yours.

It's just a birthday!

Saying you'll be there first thing Tuesday morning, doesn't in any way include the unspoken condition: '*unless* Tuesday happens to be my birthday in which case all bets are off and you can go take a flying leap'.

It's just a birthday!

When you *do* decide to turn up, several days after the appointed day, I'll be ready for you. My revenge? – '*Sorry, today's not convenient. It's the third anniversary of my dog's root canal treatment. And, as a request in advance, when you ARE here, KEEP THE FREAKIN' MUSIC DOWN!*'

SCORE = 89

By the way, in no way is my tired old brain able to compute how (as a doctor, physiotherapist etc.) it's humanly possible to be running 30 minutes late for your appointments at eight in the morning.

85.
PEOPLE WHO DON'T ACKNOWLEDGE YOUR SIMPLE ACT OF POLITENESS

85. PEOPLE WHO DON'T ACKNOWLEDGE YOUR SIMPLE ACT OF POLITENESS

The classic example is when you're driving along a narrow road or laneway and another vehicle approaches. Of course, you do what any reasonable, fair-minded person would do and pull to one side to allow the other vehicle to pass.

You'd well imagine that in a civilised society an acknowledgement of your selfless behaviour would be forthcoming from the other driver. Falling down adulation is unnecessary (as we know), as is an over exaggerated mouthing of 'THANK YOU!'

But the bozo in the other car not only doesn't acknowledge your act of politeness with so much as the one-finger-raised-from-the-steering-wheel wave, he or she ignorantly sails past with not so much as a cursory acknowledgement. Not even a quick nod of the head. In fact, there's usually no eye contact made at all.

Such blatant rudeness (even if it also demonstrates ignorance and/or embarrassment)!

If I had the time, or could think quickly enough (and, unfortunately, I never can), I'd give my own one-finger wave, but would deploy the middle finger as my digit of choice.

SCORE = 91

P.S. How our dear young friend Rebekkkkkkahh copes when she confronts in the supermarket aisle our equally yummy mummy Tiffany (power pramming young Rage) doesn't bear thinking.

It's a clash of the titans, if not heavyweights. There can only be one winner. My money's on Bekkkkkk.

86.
KNOWING BUGGER ALL ABOUT THE NEW JOB YOU JUST STARTED

Sadly, I've been in this position many times.

Note for file: When you've absolutely no clue what to do next in a new job, just storm around the office looking very serious, with a permanent scowl, and shake your head a lot. You either look as if you know what you're doing, or appear important, or both, if you perform convincingly enough. Works a treat.

By the way, it also helps if you carry a large wodge of paper around with you (doesn't matter what's on it or whether anything's on it) and mumble to yourself things like 'bunch of fucking cowboys!' At the very least, people leave you alone. That's always a plus. It's remarkable how many plainly intimidated souls approach you thereafter with the words: 'Sorry to bother you …'

This is not just a half-baked theory, folks.

I've put in into practice and I'm here to tell you it actually works!

SCORE = 83

P.S. Don't forget. Always, always, always have an Excel spreadsheet displayed on your computer screen, and a bar chart, pie chart, flow chart (which, incidentally, are impossible for me to follow) or graph on your *second* screen. Even if, like me, you don't have the foggiest idea how to interpret them, let alone how to actually create one.

Remember, guys, it's all about perception and image. *Nothing else matters.*

87.
2:29.42 AM AND THE BRAIN/BLADDER HOSTILITIES

This one *literally* pisses me off.

It's no contest. The bladder wins hands down every time – please excuse the disturbing mixed metaphor.

Maybe it's an age thing, but I can't remember the last time I slept through the night, uninterrupted by the impossibly irresistible necessity to remove myself from a warm, comfy bed to pee.

In the process, I routinely:

- *Crack my right shin on the lounge room coffee table;*
- *Head butt the fridge;*
- *Accidentally activate the car alarm;*
- *Tread on the TV remote, thereby exposing myself to the 326th re-run of* The Bill;
- *Accidentally activate the double garage roller door (which hasn't worked for the last three months);*
- *Somehow, mistakenly find myself in the next-door neighbour's back garden peeing on their prize-winning orchid display (for some weird reason, the prized orchids look distinctly more like Triffids this year); and*
- *Finally, arrive back at my now ice-chilled bed about two hours later, having tramped 10kms around the neighbourhood (where was Siri when I needed her?), just in time for my alarm to go off – three hours prematurely – and desperately needing another pee.*

SCORE = 90

88.
TRIAL BY MEDIA AND THE ARMCHAIR JUDGMENT

Sadly, we live in a society that's all too willing to cast judgment, and then dispense what it believes to be appropriate justice, on those who it deems have done wrong. Retribution is administered with almost gladiatorial fervour. The wrongdoer is stripped bare, unceremoniously hauled over the coals, and more often than not, branded (by the media in particular) with the 'disgraced' or 'failed' tag for evermore.

We're content to inflict a convenient, armchair judgment. An instant referendum, so-called.

The result is, too often, a permanent shackle around the wrongdoer's neck. Or, an invisible ball and chain that's irremovably manacled to their ankle.

The wrongdoer experiences the awful feeling of being the unintended victim of a high school science experiment. Like an insect specimen pinned prostrate on a microscope slide having its limbs coldly, systematically and callously yanked from each bodily socket. And, then being dissected by a razor-sharp scalpel until its innards have been spilt onto a petri dish for all the world to gawk at and deride.

How many different forms of punishment need to be metered out and endured? Isn't one enough for most 'crimes'?

88. TRIAL BY MEDIA AND THE ARMCHAIR JUDGMENT

We're quick to judge and even quicker to hang.
And quicker still to deny a right of redemption.

SCORE = 96

P.S. None of the above applies to Trump.

89.
MEETINGS AND THE PEOPLE WHO ATTEND THEM

89. MEETINGS AND THE PEOPLE WHO ATTEND THEM

I've found over a 45-year-plus working life (that's still going, regrettably) that most meetings seem to exist for their own sake and are, in any case, little more than glorified pissing contests. And, I'm not sure where the glory part comes in. I've also found that the vast majority of meetings (except for those that are cancelled) actually achieve very little, particularly the ones I've chaired myself.

On a scale of 1–10 of things I dislike, meetings would have to score 843. But, just maybe, it's *me*.

As we know, there's a committee for every endeavour these days and, hence, multiple meetings to go with it. A meeting invitation will be sent out to the (interim) committee members and it'll take about three months before a suitable time and date can be found to convene. At least two members of the committee will be unavailable at the last minute (having another meeting that clashes) and another three months will elapse before another suitable time and date are found.

If/when a meeting is scheduled and finally held, the inevitable pissing contest will ensue with each and every (interim) committee member having their say, just because they can, expressing their opinions, flexing their muscles, bringing all sorts of irrelevant rubbish 'to the table', puffing out their chests and otherwise wasting everyone else's time.

Nothing substantive will be decided at the (interim) meeting, but general agreement will be reached, after a heated two-hour discussion, on the time/date/venue for the next (interim) meeting.

Minutes of the (interim) meeting will be circulated for comment. There'll be many comments, more than at the actual meeting, but no agreement reached on the content of the minutes, thus confirming that not only was there nothing of importance decided at the meeting, but also that no (interim) committee member was able to agree whether the meeting was actually held or that they had actually attended.

A dispute will nevertheless erupt on whether the (interim) minutes constitute a fair and reasonable account of what transpired at the (interim) meeting, thus reinforcing the view held by a two-thirds majority of the (interim) committee members (thankfully a 'quorum'), that no discussion had in fact taken place on the (interim) agenda items. (Time was of the essence at the time and the time simply ran out because the [interim] meeting room was double-booked.)

But surprisingly, the (interim) committee was able to find *some* common ground and tabled the following for consideration at the first *official* committee meeting to be held in six months time, which, as it happens, falls on Christmas Day:

- *That the (interim) committee Chair should be sanctioned for using an imitation Darth Vader light saber as her whiteboard pointer.*

99. MEETINGS AND THE PEOPLE WHO ATTEND THEM

- *That young Marigold and Xander should in future refrain from making out when the meeting room lights are dimmed for a video presentation.*
- *That an investigation will be undertaken immediately into the identity and conduct of the unnamed and unknown person who vacated the meeting after announcing, two hours into the meeting: 'I'm terribly sorry, I've just realised I'm in the wrong meeting.' (Particularly as that person was elected as the [interim] meeting minute-taker and buggered off with the [interim] meeting notes.)*
- *That the Chair should be further reprimanded, and placed on (interim) probation, for ending the (interim) committee meeting with the words: 'Guys, make it happen!'*
- *That the use of multiple 'woo woos' is an unacceptable means of achieving consensus and recording (interim) committee decisions.*

SCORE = 99

90.
THE UBIQUITOUS 'COFFEE TRAVELLER'

90. THE UBIQUITOUS 'COFFEE TRAVELLER'

Please tell me I'm wrong, but is there anyone left on this planet who's capable of navigating their way through even a microsecond of the day without a mug (the eco-friendly designer/non-disposable variety of course) of skinny milk/mocha/frappé/affogato/dolce/macchiato/turmeric latte permanently embedded in their paw?

They march into work with them, stride confidently (usually misplaced) with keep cup in hand to and from the 27 pointless meetings they'll attend during the day. They even take them to and from the catch-up coffee with the bestie.

- Wanky fashion statement for some? Undoubtedly.
- An essential 'help-me-make-it-through-the-day' infusion of caffeine for others? Unquestionably.
- A conscious look-at-me moment to demonstrate to the world that 'I'm just too busy to stop'? Clearly.
- A subconscious emotional prop for the tragically unaware? Of course.
- An unthinking reflex action by the vast majority? Roger that.

SCORE = 82

P.S. Have I ever committed this daft practice myself for any of the above reasons? You betcha!

Hence, the relatively pitiable score. I let myself off lightly.

91.
'SO, HOW'S YOUR DAY BEEN SO FAR?'

91. 'SO, HOW'S YOUR DAY BEEN SO FAR?'

Doesn't this one give you the screaming you-know-whats?

It makes me feel like dragging that pair of heavy-duty pliers out of the toolbox and administering some rough justice. If I could only figure out how *they* work, too.

The question is usually, but not exclusively, delivered by a thirteen-year-old-looking check out chick/chuck at the local supermarket or bank. It's spat out in a tone and with a glazed-over-the-eyes expression (and forced smiley face) that reinforces the impression that the question is being asked with as much genuine enthusiasm and sincerity as an enquiry about the present state of your prostate condition.

It's a dead giveaway that the question has been plucked straight from the mental Rolodex (Item No. 47) when our young friends get the words muddled up: *'So, day how's been so your far?'*

SCORE = 75: A RELATIVELY LOW PISSED-OFF SCORE AS I APPRECIATE THAT OUR YOUNG FRIENDS ARE ONLY TRYING (PROBABLY AT THE INSISTENCE OF THEIR BOSS AND/OR THE RELEVANT FAST FOOD/BANK CADET TRAINEE INDUCTION PROGRAM [KNOWN BY THE NOW INDUSTRY-ACCEPTED BUZZ EXPRESSION 'C-TIP']) TO BE FRIENDLY.

They've just picked the wrong person to be friendly to. And, most likely, the wrong time of the day.

92.
THE WANKY HEALTH AND FITNESS INDUSTRY

92. THE WANKY HEALTH AND FITNESS INDUSTRY

(I think I might be in a little bit of bother on this one.)

And now for some miscellaneous and not so complimentary observations about the rubbish/pretentious/narcissistic/wanky health and fitness industry.

You'll be well aware by now that I'm not the sort of person who exercises in order to 'make a statement' appearance-wise. I don't preen, primp, prance, ponce, pose or pretend. There's no escaping the sad and undeniable fact that I've irreversibly achieved crusty, broken-down, old-fart status.

My once chiseled features (OK, *feature* – wherever it hid itself) have now taken on the appearance of having been mercilessly pummeled by a sledgehammer. My abs, pecks and glutes have all gone MIA, notwithstanding that I've always had difficulty locating them in the first place. I'm now less 'ripped' and more completely in tatters.

I certainly don't run to satisfy some perverse gear fetish either, as many seem to these days. I run in the same gear until it literally falls apart, which it has, embarrassingly, on a number of occasions. And I'm talking pants slipping half-mast at the midway point of a marathon. (Actually, that's happened twice now – at the *same* race, but 34 years apart! True story.)

For about twenty years, I ran in the same crappy blue cap that's only recently been retired because it begged me to 'let it go'. I still have it though. I don't have the heart to bury or cremate it. In any case, it'd probably return to terrorise me, *Pet Sematary*-style.

Incidentally, I don't fast (no discipline). I don't belong to a gym (noise/crowds/wankers). I won't (read: can't) pump, static stretch, bench press or participate in HIIT. I don't, at the end of a run, bellow out a primal scream (way too self-conscious and couldn't summon the required energy). I save that inclination for other more appropriate moments. Like when politicians try to sound sincere, but only end up sounding evangelical. (When you're exceedingly busy, even if you're achieving very little, I guess it's easy to get Sunday muddled up with the other days of the week.)

I'm also not into diets (unwavering skepticism/inability to commit): gluten-free, Paleo, Ketogenic, Atkins, 5:2, South Beach or otherwise. And finally, I don't indulge in one of the wankiest practices (un)known to the health and fitness industry: I don't exercise with a water bottle. OMG. Shock horror.

Apologies to all those who do (well, not really), but what an overblown extravagance that is. Why would you need a slug of water at the end of every second lap of the pool? Why would you need to stop and drink every five minutes in the gym? Why would you have a water bottle strapped to your side on a leisurely morning stroll around the lake in the middle of winter?

C'mon guys, get real. Yeah, OK, fluid intake is important. I get that. But, if you need hydration, why not thoroughly hydrate *before* and re-hydrate *after* you exercise. Surely, that's sufficient?

92. THE WANKY HEALTH AND FITNESS INDUSTRY

To my admittedly very unprofessional eye (but still, a 40 year plus running 'career'), very few forms of exercise require such a significant amount of *continual* re-hydration. Ultramarathon running and other ultra-sporting events would be exceptions. Likewise, cyclists generally only carry water bottles because they're on their bikes for two hours plus, and simply because they can.

And, do we really need to be sucking on a water bottle *all* day, even in the office?

It's a vastly overblown practice in my view.

Or is it just *me*?

SCORE = 91

93.
BEING HOPELESSLY UNFIT

93. BEING HOPELESSLY UNFIT

Despite my rather offbeat and plainly out-of-step attitude to exercise (and just about everything else, let's be honest), fitness is still hugely important to me. I loathe being unfit.

As mentioned, I've been a runner/someone who runs for over 40 years. In that time, I reckon I've run close to 100,000 kilometres, or the equivalent of about 2.5 times around the planet. And though it's true to say I've often been disrespectful to it, running has been a true and loyal friend to me in that time.

I've run around Central Park in New York. I've run around Lake Geneva and Lake Burley Griffin. I've run multiple laps of a concrete velodrome in Rosebery (north west Tasmania) in pitch darkness. I've run around the Bathurst motor racing circuit. I've run in the chaos of Bangkok and the tranquility of a Queensland rainforest. I've run on the Royal Canberra Golf Course, the MCG and Adelaide Oval. I've run over the Yorkshire moors in freezing sleet. I've run in Darwin in the middle of the monsoon season. I've run in the scorching Pilbara summer heat (even in the dead of night). I've run through snow in Vienna and through snow in Perisher Valley. I've run around Parliament House in protest. I've even run to the 'Edge of the World' and back.

I'm by no means a fitness fanatic. Nevertheless, I detest that depressing and demoralising feeling of being an unhealthy lump of sludge through lack of exercise. I need say no more on the subject. Quite simply, being unfit pisses me off, chronically, at an out-of-control rage level. Being horribly unfit at present, you'll understand why I'm particularly grumpy right here, right now.

SCORE = 95

94.
PEOPLE WHO INSIST ON 'MAKING A STATEMENT'

I have to be a bit careful here as this one saddens me as much as I find it truly irritating.

Personally, I have no inclination to make a statement (possibly because I feel I have little that's meaningful enough to make a statement about, apart from the endless ramblings in this book) and have a huge problem with people who do, merely for the sake of it. Especially when the statement they're making is of no significance or importance to any person on the planet other than themselves. And, that's a stretch.

I've already mentioned my inability to comprehend why there are those in society who regard fashion, and the curious tendency to parade around in the most idiotic ensembles, as a means of making a significant, life-changing personal statement. For what purpose? To convey an impression? To promote an image? Sounds a bit shallow when you dig beneath the surface and pose some obvious questions.

Stranger still to me, is the weird inclination that many people have to make a statement in the building of a house.

I can understand well enough that, through ingenious design and the clever use of space, sensible and sensitive architecture can be an instrument of positive social change. Clever architecture *can* put humanity back into buildings, as I've heard it said. But, to me at least, a vastly different scenario results when the construction

94. PEOPLE WHO INSIST ON 'MAKING A STATEMENT'

of a house descends into little more than an ego-driven extravagance.

Tell me:
- *Is it a house or, in truth, a homage?*
- *If a house is a reflection of personality, it's troubling to me that so many houses are ugly monstrosities*
- *If a house carries a 'personal signature', what does that say about the owners of so many jarring blots on the landscape?*
- *If a house says something about who you are, what does that say about the owners of a house bearing a cluttered interior full of junk?*

It's a house.

Its superficial appeal and whatever trinkets and embellishments it contains (that often showcase no more than elegant or up market poverty), are surely far less important than functionality, best use of space, utility and environmental sustainability. And, even more importantly you'd think, how lives are lived on the inside.

I'm no psychologist, but don't those who possess a bursting need to 'make a statement' (about anything quite frankly) merely paper over a deeply felt sense of insecurity and inadequacy?

Take a leaf out my book. You can feel exactly the same without having to make a statement about it. It's totally unnecessary guys.

Stop trying so hard.

You're as perfect as you need to be.

In any case, guess what? Like the sound of one hand clapping, no one can hear you.

SCORE = 93

95.
THE UNREALITY OF REALITY TV

I'd be the first tribal member to be turfed on *Survivor*.

Come to think of it, I'd probably volunteer to go. The tribe wouldn't be compelled to 'speak'. I'd gladly give up the immunity idol for a one-way ticket out. Either that or I'd pitch a tent on the opposite side of the island and secretly raid the other camp at midnight. In any case, the whole crowd/tribe thing would likely be too much for me, I strongly suspect.

Reality TV? We're talking a contradiction in terms here, aren't we? How can something pass for 'reality' when it's plainly artificial, contrived, heavily stage-managed and carefully choreographed? It's less to do with reality and more to do with a massively out-of-proportion 'look at me' opportunity. It has little to do with reality and everything to do with a theatrical performance, minus the talent factor of either 'playwright' or 'actor'.

It is 'spontaneity', after 27 takes. It presents things 'as they happened', after days of obvious, painstaking rehearsal.

On these shows the worse you behave, the bigger 'star' you become. In reality, however, very few of the participants survive the experience with any degree of self-respect, dignity or credibility. The sad reality is how much Reality TV highlights overwhelming ordinariness.

C'mon, admit it, even if you're hooked. It's lazy, junk entertainment that has zero substance. It's trashy froth-and-bubble designed to wash over you, audiovisual junk food to be digested without thought or effort. It's

95. THE UNREALITY OF REALITY TV

unashamedly not meant to intellectually stimulate or educate. It's a quick fix fill-in; a foot-long meatball sub; the TV version of the Happy Meal.

These shows are about as personally satisfying as drinking flat, warm beer. Or skim milk.

And, once they're over, if you're anything like me (okay, that's unlikely), you can't help thinking that you've been monumentally conned.

Or in need of a quick shower.

Or both.

SCORE = 94

P.S. The only concession I'll make is that Reality TV is infinitely more entertaining and believable than Question Time on any typical parliamentary sitting day. State or federal.

96.
FOODIE WANKERS: LOOKING GOOD ON TV AND BEING ABLE TO BOIL AN EGG

96. FOODIE WANKERS

Amongst a number of previous lives, personal reinventions and reincarnations, there was a time when I worked as a cook in a seafood restaurant in Venus Bay, Victoria. Long story.

To be clear, during my time at The Fishing Village Bar & Cafe (Grump Tavern as I secretly knew it), I was certainly no TV celebrity chef, who, these days, is really anybody who looks attractive on TV and can boil an egg. I fail miserably at the former and can only barely navigate the latter without some kind of minor catastrophe.

It goes without saying that I was no Heston Blumenthal. More like a cross between Rick Stein and Greasy Joe – but more Joe than Rick. I never seriously considered changing my professional name to Chef Rosco and/or cultivating a Neil Perry-like ponytail. Although I dare say that may've attracted a few more punters and, after all, I also knew a few French phrases from high school. And, at times, my very ordinary, grump-flavoured kitchen language would've even made Gordon Ramsay cringe.

Our very modest cafe was never going to be awarded a Chef's Hat or make it into the Michelin restaurant guide. No matter how much you dress it up, and dress it up we did, fish and chips is never going to cut it as 'techno-emotional cuisine'. We were never going to be awarded a Global Dining Oscar either. The food on our simple menu wasn't a fusion of Australian and Asian flavours or a fusion of anything actually, particularly not science and art.

Neither was it by any means 'eclectic', nor did it fit neatly into a well-defined 'genre'. There was no French, Italian, Greek, nouveau Scando/Japanese or traditional Mongolian element to it. We didn't serve snail porridge, or edible tinsel, which, apparently, you could dine on at Heston's joint at one time.

Deconstructed coffee? Syringe-infused pastries? Eating food as an 'event'? There was none of that.

No, as a cook, I was neither innovative nor particularly inventive. With absolutely no formal cooking qualifications, and very little practical experience, I just hung on by the skin of my teeth and hoped like hell I'd get through each day.

Out of pure necessity, our rather naïve approach was to serve good, tasty food at a reasonable price and I think we got it right.

Such heresy. How dare we trivialise the culinary experience.

I know it's a terrible admission but, really folks, it's only food in my view. It's not an art form, at least, needless to say, it wasn't with me. To me, food (like life generally) doesn't warrant over-analysis or over-complication. And that's especially the case when it comes to seafood. Good seafood needs little help to enhance it. It certainly doesn't deserve to be manipulated with every imaginable sauce or spice that drowns or overpowers its natural taste. Like life, it is what it is, or should be.

Rick might agree, Joe definitely would, but I suspect

few others out there in restaurant world.

It seems much easier to perpetuate the myth and make cooking look harder or more complicated than it needs to be. The result is that we tend to give up in frustration and retreat to our time-honoured and foolproof favourites like spag bol or mince on toast. Nothing wrong with either, in my book, though.

Fine dining? Nonsense. Forget it. Once a week chicken and chips with heaps of gravy and peas (and a banana fritter if indulgence is your thing)? Worth every penny.

SCORE = 96

P.S. A note to all you professional foodie cooks out there: Please stop shoving your nose to within 2 millimetres of the plate as you apply the finishing touches, with your nifty pair of tweezers or mini squirt bottle, to one of your 'creations'.

It's a plate of food, goddammit, not microscopic brain surgery, and nowhere near as significant, or life changing, or important.

Such a wanky affectation!

Keep it real!

97.
SELFIES AND GRINNING GOOSES

97. SELFIES AND GRINNING GOOSES

SCORE = SORRY, NO GUESSES FOR THIS ONE

98.
THE GRINDING HUMILIATION OF UNEMPLOYMENT

98. THE GRINDING HUMILIATION OF UNEMPLOYMENT

For an almost three-year period from late 2014, I made literally hundreds of unsuccessful attempts to find employment and had reached the point where I'd virtually given up job hunting as a forlorn and fruitless lost cause. (The age factor didn't help.) Without being conscious of it, I'd taken the concept of casualisation to a new and depressing level. I'd become, inadvertently, a full-time 'permalancer'. CEO at Unemployed Inc.

There is a lighter side, however, even to the mind-numbing hopelessness of being unemployed. You may be intrigued to learn that at one stage I became an official Newstart claimant. Thereafter, I became known simply as 'Jobseeker 0365494019'.

At one point, I had my 'participation interview' by phone with a wonderfully dedicated young fellow from Centrelink who, by the conclusion of our chat, was highly embarrassed that the pro forma questionnaire that he ran through was in no way relevant to me or my qualifications and experience. However, we pressed on and, by the end, we'd become great pals.

The next day, I ventured to a Centrelink office, this time for a face-to-face interview with an equally kind soul. I sought advice from my kids on how I should present myself.

My truly amazing, multi-talented son, Hamish, was particularly forthcoming:

Dad, correct me if I'm wrong.

One aim here is to get as many benefits as you can for as long as you can, until such time as you actually find work (a 'job' in itself). You must realise that you're now walking a tightrope, and a thin one at that. Don't try hard enough, consequence = no benefits. Try too hard, consequence = you may, indeed, be found a job, though I appreciate this is your ultimate, and preferred, aim. I suggest a middle ground, somewhere between mild confidence and early onset dementia. Shouldn't be too hard for you.

Shaving only half your face, shirt buttons in non-opposing holes, loose-fitting belt, frayed cuffs, badly polished shoes and a little dab of either mustard or tomato sauce strategically placed on your tie. (Both would be going a bit too far.) Consider seeking out the older, heavy set lady in the Centrelink office. The one wearing a green cardigan with reading glasses attached to a chain around her neck. And, usually occupying a workstation towards the rear of the room adjacent to the toilet.

Stopping at the local bakery, I suggest purchasing one éclair and one custard-filled, not jam (too sweet), donut. Present it to her upon arrival, just to

98. THE GRINDING HUMILIATION OF UNEMPLOYMENT

let her know how much you appreciate and value her help during this difficult transition.

Seriously, unemployment sucks.

SCORE = 94

P.S. I broke through my own personal unemployment glass ceiling in September 2017. Someone, oddly, saw something in me worthwhile. Even though, at 65, I was so far past ripe old age I was starting to rot.

And the low hanging fruit was beginning to fall off.

99.
CATHETER TUBES AND HOW NOT TO INSTALL THEM

99. CATHETER TUBES AND HOW NOT TO INSTALL THEM

Aren't they meant to take the piss, not piss you off?

In early November 2014, while driving to pick up Mrs B from a medical appointment in Perth, I was cleaned up by a five tonne truck on Mounts Bay Road near Kings Park.

Shit happened, right on cue.

The truck hit me side on, T-bone style. The only comment the completely unscathed boofhead truck driver could offer was: *'Didn't see ya mate'*.

No shit?

When the ambulance arrived, my neck was placed in a brace and I was hauled off to the nearby Sir Charles Gairdner Hospital. At that point, I can only remember being jumped on by a squad of attentive doctors and hospital staff in the Emergency Department, where I had my clothes scissored off and tubes and other assorted gadgets attached to, or inserted into, various body parts that seemed in need of a moderate dose of care and attention.

Anyway, to cut short a long and painful story, I was discharged four days later with a few fractured vertebrae in my neck, several cracked ribs and some miscellaneous plumbing issues.

Please don't mention the 'c word' here, though, 'catheter', that is. For many weeks after the crash, I could still see the horrible wee pee tube whenever I closed my eyes. That reaction might've had something to do with the 'Nurse Ratched' who gleefully inserted it into me, after several false starts, when I couldn't perform without her rough handling, as it were. The least she could've done was to enquire whether it'd been 'good for me too'.

It hadn't. And I continue to be wary of hospitals as well as nurses with glints in their eyes, especially those who chirp that 'this won't hurt a bit'.

Or, who casually throw in the double meaning 'just a little prick' comment seconds before they do just that.

SCORE = 89

100.
THE PERFORMING NOSE SYNDROME

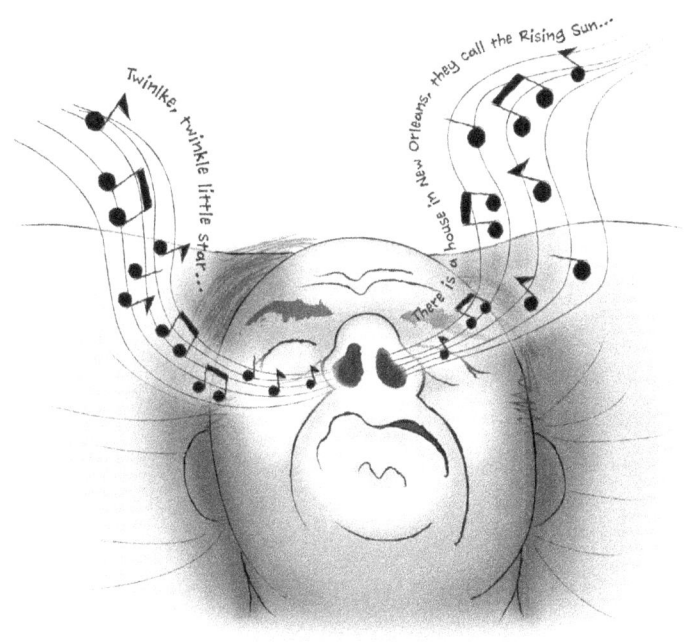

Picture the scene, if you dare. And to make it much easier for you to comprehend, let's cast a past event in the present tense.

I'm laying in bed minding my own business. Maybe that's where the problem begins. All's quiet.

Just as I'm about to nod off and drift into blissful slumber, the nostrils begin to do their thing. First the right (despite being almost permanently blocked after multiple broken noses) and, at precisely the wrong time, the left. In perfect synchronisation and harmony, they commence their extensive repertoire – which includes any tune from *Beethoven's Fifth Symphony* to 'Twinkle, Twinkle Little Star'.

Sometimes, each nostril will perform a solo, as if to give their colleague a short but much-needed rest – maybe a toilet break. Inevitably, however, they're much happier performing together, occasionally in 'duelling banjos' fashion.

Whether in unison or going it alone, it makes diddly squat difference. The end result pisses me off beyond belief. No matter what I do – rub either nostril, give the whole snoz a vigorous shake or, in a state of complete exasperation, plant one or more fingers up either or both nostrils thereby inducing a catastrophic nosebleed – I only ever succeed in changing the tone or the pitch of the unwanted recital.

100. THE PERFORMING NOSE SYNDROME

I only, finally, fall asleep from sheer exhaustion after humming along for three hours to the *Hallelujah Chorus* or the first three verses of 'Stairway to Heaven'.

Thirty minutes after finally falling asleep: See Thing 87.

SCORE = 92

A FINAL (GRUMPY) WORD

OK, you're done. You made it.

I trust the 'journey' wasn't too painful or heart wrenching for you. I trust you don't feel outraged or dragged down by my negativity or my cynical Dismal Dick view of the world to the point where you seriously doubt, or like me don't care, whether you'll make it out of bed tomorrow morning.

Grossly offensive? No doubt, to some. Didn't pass the pub test? Very likely. Didn't pass the political correctness test? I certainly hope so. Lecturing and sanctimonious? If so, definitely unintended, but I'll wear the criticism. More likely, though, just plain grumpy, which makes it relatively easy to take a giant swipe at the world, and a few sacred cows, at the same time. (Except, of course, those that produce the milk with the dollop.)

I'll leave you to make the call on that one.

What about a book on all the things that make me happy, I hear you ask? I'll get back to you on that. I'll email you if/when I think of any. Don't expect a text.

Anyway, thanks for coming. Though, whether you made it to this point or gave up in revulsion, despair or complete indifference, I really don't give a toss, as you know.

A FINAL (GRUMPY) WORD

KEEP IT REAL!

GRUMPS RULE!

WOO WOO!

* * *

P.S. I'm accepting suggestions for Volume Two. Get *your* people to call *my* people. We'll do lunch. I'm thinking: *100 Things that Piss Me Off (Volume Two) – the Musical*. A sequel to the prequel to the sequel? Maybe I'll franchise it? The possibilities, obviously, are endless.

Contenders for Volume Two include:

Not being able to choose any dish from a restaurant menu (Er, on second thoughts, lunch might be a bit tricky)

....

TV interviewers who prefer the sound of their own voice

....

The compulsory hug and cheek-bump greeting

....

That life seems to be getting harder

....

100 THINGS THAT PISS ME OFF

The misuse of the word 'marathon'

Always being in the wrong queue

Animals dressed up as humans

People with over-inflated egos

A fridge full of skim milk

The Mumbai call centre

Subtitled movies

The Bucket List

The Man Cave

Dog whistling

A FINAL (GRUMPY) WORD

The pub test

....

Snoring

....

Tweets

....

Emojis

....

Image

....

Noise

....

Wind

....

To contact the author, or to order further copies,
please visit: www.vividpublishing.com.au/100things

www.ingramcontent.com/pod-product-compliance
Lightning Source LLC
Chambersburg PA
CBHW031615160426
43196CB00006B/134